CAMEROON

A Lion Deeply Asleep

Linus PATEM

CAMEROON

A Lion Deeply Asleep

Building A New Cameroon

Preface by Joseph Nsom

L'Harmattan

All Scripture quotations in this work are taken from *The New Africa Bible*, published by the Paulines Publications Africa, 2011.

Imprimatur:

✠ Immanuel B. Bushu, D.Ph.

Bishop of Buea

Diocese of Buea, Cameroon

April 10, 2013

5-7, rue de l'Ecole-Polytechnique, 75005 Paris

http://www.harmattan.fr
diffusion.harmattan@wanadoo.fr
harmattan1@wanadoo.fr

ISBN : 978-2-343-06545-8
EAN : 9782343065458

"You are the light of the world.

A city set on a mountain cannot be hidden."

- *Matthew 5:14*

"I believe that if you show people the problems and you show them the solutions they will be moved to act."

- *Bill Gates*

This book is dedicated to Saint John Paul II for the greater honour and glory of God, that he may continue to intercede before Him for this country, Cameroon, which was so dear to his heart.

ACKNOWLEDGEMENTS

I am very much indebted to the staff of Anucam Educational Books Plc, Buea, for the great job they have done in preparing this manuscript for publishing. In a special way, I am thankful to Messrs Abang David and Chia Jude for their polished editorial expertise that gave this book its present form; to Mr. Asah Giles, Parish Council Chairperson of the St. John Paul II Parish Barombi-Kang, Diocese of Buea, and to Br. Cornelius Bonah, Faculty of Theology of the Catholic University of Central Africa, Yaoundé, for their valuable cooperation in proofreading great portions of the manuscript; to Mr Nsom Joseph, Ministry of Economy, Planning and Regional Development, Yaoundé, for his kindness in writing the Preface; Fr Patrick Lafon for providing me with the documents of the National Episcopal Conference of Cameroon; Professor Wilfred Ndongko of the University Institute of the Diocese of Buea (UIDB), and Mr. Lawrence Forwang, Southwest Regional Delegate of Agriculture for their kind suggestions which went a long way to improve this work.

I wish to thank in a special way my Bishop, Rt. Rev. Immanuel Bushu, Bishop of Buea, for his constant and invaluable support and encouragement. I am particularly grateful to my Professors, Rev. Fr Jean-Marie Signie, Mr. Jean-Paul Betengne, Sr. Silvia Recchi, Sr. Angele Makiang, Rev. Fr. Engelbert Meyongo, and Madam Valery Kouam all of the Department of Canon Law, Catholic University of Central Africa, Yaoundé. It would have been impossible to accomplish the task of writing this book without the exquisite tutoring I received from them which imbued me with the necessary motivation and inspiration.

May the good Lord bless them all abundantly along with all those who, though not mentioned by name, have contributed in one way or another in order to make the publication of this book possible.

I welcome suggestions for future editions of this book. After reading it, if you have suggestions, please write down your suggestion(s) and email them to me. The more complete your proposal, the more likely I will be to consider it. All suggestions that I judge will contribute significantly in making Cameroon a better nation will count. If I select your suggestion for a future edition or printing, I will surely include your name in the Acknowledgment page as a contributor to the work. Suggestions can be emailed to ***lpatem@yahoo.com.***

CONTENTS

"It is also because the Christian is faithful to the Gospel that he must engage in politics. The Christian faith is not purely something interior and private; it must extend to engagement in the social, economic, political and cultural life."

(The National Episcopal Conference of Cameroon)

"Despite occasional suggestions that there is something disloyal or unpatriotic about being vocal, critical, or contrary — we know differently. The mark of a citizen is civic engagement. It is his or her willingness to speak out and stand up; to care passionately and to have the courage to swim against the current when necessary. Doing so is nothing less than an expression of patriotism."

(HE Robert P. Jackson, Former United States Ambassador to Cameroon)

PREFACE

Cameroon, which obtained independence in 1960, is a Mid African country. From independence, the economy of Cameroon under the leadership of President Amadou Ahidjo, was guided by a five year development plan. This plan was elaborated by the Ministry of Economy and plan in consultation with the national communities. The plan explored the development aspirations of each region for a given five year period. Projects were carefully programmed within the period and inserted in the annual budgets for execution. Cameroon experienced sustained balanced growth with this development approach till the 1980s when economic crisis and alternative development strategies surfaced. The Table below shows the average period growth rates of Cameroon economy from 1980 to 2010.

Period		**Time (years)**	**Growth rate (%)**	**Observation**
1980 - 1986	A	07	+9.1	Period of great realizations
1987 – 1994	B	08	– 3.8	Period of intense multifarious crisis
1995 – 2004	C	10	+4.3	Recovery fuelled by effects of devaluation
2005 - 2010	D	06	+2.8	Global economic crisis
TOTAL	**E**	**31**	**3.0**	

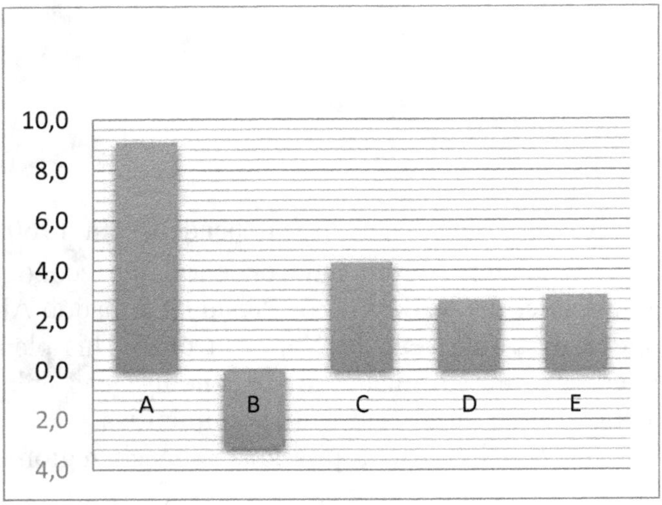

Source: *By author (data from IMF-2011 World Economic Outlook)*

The period (1980-1986) was marked by great realization in Cameroon resulting in a growth rate of 9.1%. President Paul Biya took over power in Cameroon in 1982 when Amadou Ahidjo resigned. He met several projects at the phase of implementation which he completed: the Cameroon television, the Yaoundé-Bamenda road, the Yaoundé-Douala road, ministerial buildings, etc). President Biya took over power when the economy of Cameroon was in an excellent state of health. He actually confirmed this in two of his speeches to the nation in the following words, and I quote *"Je dis sans embage que l'économie du Cameroun se porte très bien"*, meaning *"I say with certainty that the Cameroon economy is doing very well"*. In the year 1986, he officially informed Cameroonians of an *"economic crisis"* which subsequently generated other crisis.

The crisis, which first surfaced by 1986, had internal and external causes. Internally, the Cameroon economy was characterized by acute mismanagement of resources, lack of vision as well as planning. Externally, there was a fall in the prices of export products (cocoa, coffee, rubber, banana, cotton etc) which resulted in a drastic drop in export earnings. This crisis visited all the countries whose main export earnings were from these products.

Well managed economies reacted to this crisis by adjusting their macroeconomic equilibrium to suit the prevailing situation. Cameroon, a poorly managed economy reacted by inviting the Bretton Woods Institution's for assistance. By 1988, a Structural Adjustment Programme (SAP) was introduced in Cameroon by the Bretton Woods Institutions (IMF and World Bank). This put an end to the five year development plan that existed since independence. From this period, the economic policy in Cameroon was managed virtually by these institutions. In 1993, draconian economic measures were applied in the Cameroon public sector - salaries of civil servants were slashed by more than 50%, several services and industries were closed down resulting in a general retrenchment of workers. As if this was not enough, the Franc CFA was devalued by 50% in 1994. No accompanying measures followed this devaluation as was the case elsewhere in the CFA franc zone.

One of the most astonishing behaviour observed during that period was that Cameroonians did not manifest any dissatisfaction against these draconian measures. They swallowed these very bitter pills and remained submissive throughout the difficult period. From this unexplained behavior, the government understood that Cameroonians were predisposed to bearing any burden imposed on them. This gave them a very comfortable position to manipulate Cameroon and Cameroonians at any time and in any manner.

For a period of 31 years, i.e. from 1980 to 2010, Cameroon registered an average economic growth rate of 3%, as against an average population growth rate of 2.7% over the same period. This implies that the economic welfare of

Cameroonians deteriorated significantly over this period. There are no clear prospects for any amelioration in the future. Poverty and endemic corruption have settled comfortably in virtually all the sectors of the economy, and there is ample evidence that this situation will be sustained in the long run. The authorities are trying to mask this reality with the popular assertion that Cameroon will emerge in 2035. What evidence do we have today to project a change in such a distant future? By the way, what do we understand by an emerging country?

Understanding the Notion of Emerging Nations

Initially, the world countries were classified into two main groups – developed and developing countries. In the course of time some developing nations developed their economies to a stage that placed them somewhere between the developed and developing countries. At that level, they are growing to the stage of developed countries. They are said to be emerging from the stage of developing economies to that of developed economies.

Originally brought into fashion in the 80s by the then World Bank economist Antoine Van Agtmael, the word *"emerging nations"* describes the process of those developing countries undergoing sustained high economic growth, industrialization and acquisition of significant shares in world trade.

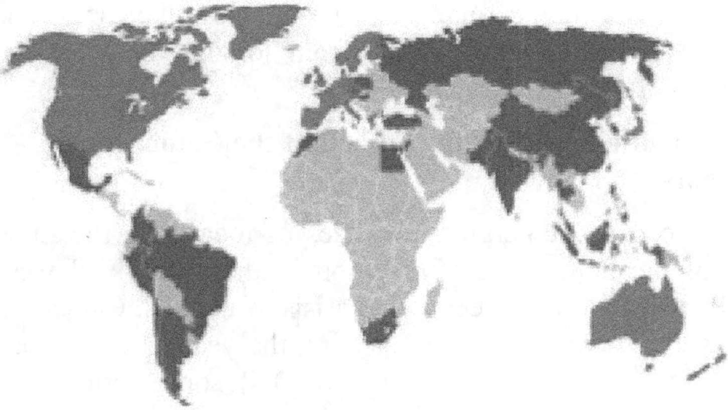

Classification of world countries today.

"Emerging country" is an elusive concept, as we may not say how much emergence is needed for a nation to move from developing to developed. China remains an emerging nation despite its second position as the largest world economy after the USA.

The emerging countries are classified by generation, with the first generation grouping those nations which are at the verge of joining the developed countries. Majority of the nations in the first generation come from Asia (China, Korea, India, Malaysia, Thailand…) and Latin America (Brazil, Argentina, Chile…) with only the Republic of South Africa in Africa. The second generation is focused on – Bangladesh, Tunisia, Costa Rica, Egypt, Sri Lanka, Mauritius, Morocco etc. The third generation stares at some countries in Africa: Mozambique, Nigeria, Kenya, Ghana, Senegal, Botswana, Rwanda, Malawi and Mauritius. Cameroon is still to find its generation, but it is already known by the politicians that it could emerge in 2035. What are those problems that are hindering this mighty giant, Cameroon, described by some persons as *"the sleeping lion"* from joining the world of progress?

3. Factors hindering the takeoff of the Cameroon Economy

The so called emerging countries of today had the same level of development as Cameroon in the 1960s and were equally affected by the economic crisis of the 80s. Cameroon could have been at least approaching the year of emergence today (at least the second generation) if some seriousness existed in the way state affairs were managed. Since the 80s, Cameroonians have been living like thieves in their own houses, with individuals in positions of power confiscating virtually all what belongs to the society. Several scenarios do exist which actually hinder the progress of Cameroon in almost all domains of human activity.

i) Permanent absence of Vision and Planning

Today, Cameroon is a low profile agricultural country despite its huge natural potentialities and resources. These represent great investment opportunities. Natural resources are abundant throughout the country – primary products, waters, forests, mines, fertile lands, waterfalls etc. Most of these resources are either lying idle, under-utilized or poorly managed. The agricultural sector as a whole has not acquired the necessary momentum needed to harness and sustain food production for the population. The industrial sector has experienced significant decline since the 90s. Several state enterprises throughout the national territory were either closed down or rendered inefficient as a result of poor management. The various sectors of the Cameroon economy have not been given the attention needed to respond to the increasing growing needs of the economy.

With a population of about 20 million persons today as against 5 millions in the 60s, the productive capacities of the primary and secondary sectors of production have not undergone any significant changes in the course of time. Cameroon has intensified the importation of basic food commodities (rice, corn and fish) in recent years despite the potentials available all over the national territory for increased production. A permanent absence of vision and planning are responsible for this situation. Authorities are not aware of this situation, and we may be sleeping on a timed bomb if this unfortunate situation is not adequately addressed.

ii) Laxity and Inertia – a way of life in Cameroon

Cameroon has a highly centralized government. All the essential powers of the state are concentrated in Yaoundé, the political capital. The ten regions which compose Cameroon are simply the wings of the central authority in Yaoundé. The governors who head these regions as well as the Ministers in the central administration are the authorities to whom political power has been delegated by the head of state. They are responsible for running the daily affairs of Cameroon in all the areas of human activities.

The Cameroon of today is what these authorities made of it yesterday, and the Cameroon of tomorrow shall be what these authorities shall make of it today. These authorities are essentially administrative in the way they operate as opposed to managerial. The manager is an administrator with an objective to initiate and create something. He or she is at the centre of decision making. The administrator functions on the instructions of the boss, and may not initiate anything at his or her level.

These administrators are there to serve more the interest of the Boss (head of state) than that of the state and so most of the time they tend to sit and wait for instructions from the

Boss. The head of state has decried this attitude several times in his speeches. He qualifies this attitude of his collaborators as inertia and yet no real measures have been put in place to change the situation. For most actions undertaken by these administrators, they relate them to instructions coming from the head of state, meaning of course that they do not initiate anything at their level.

There is little or no creativity, as these administrators are not obliged to produce any concrete results. Very little or no attention is given to the realization of projects earmarked in the budget. For most projects initiated in the public sector, administrative procedures and formalities (seminars, missions, entertainment etc.) tend to consume most of the time and money needed to execute the project. Excessive bureaucracy and corruption actually hinder the realization of most projects in the public sector in Cameroon.

iii) The Government cares more for Individuals to the detriment of the State

People appointed to positions of authority in Cameroon tend to consider such appointments more as favours made to them by the head of state than as appointments based on merit and competence. Consequently, they tend to concentrate more on lip service and writing messages of unconditional support to the head of state than on the job they are paid to do. In order words, the interest of the state is somehow put aside while that of the boss is projected. After the cabinet shakeup of 10th December 2011, one of the members of government in Cameroon put it in this way, and I quote.

> "*I do not have any account to render to the Cameroonian people. I was appointed by Biya. I depend on him, I am answerable to him and I render my account only to him*".

The boss on the other hand projects the interests of his collaborators by the toleration of the system of impunity in which they operate. They do all what they like with the resources put at their disposal, and most of them go scot free after misusing such resources. They live in an artificial affluent society, completely in contrast with the ordinary Cameroon society.

The amount of resources used to comfort a (Minister or Director General) and all the others in related positions can be disturbing if we consider the famous alibi (economic crisis) always put forward by these authorities to justify the non-provision of the most essential needs in Cameroon. These people are entitled to everything that a human being may need. In addition to their salary they have allowances for (fuel, water, electricity, telephone, etc) and all the other allowances as often indicated in the famous "Article 2" which reads: "*Les intéressés auront droits aux avantages de toute nature prévus par la réglementation en vigueur.*[1]"

In highly productive systems like the United Nations, World Bank, IMF and the others, similar advantages will accrue to individuals in managerial positions. In such systems, the aims of high financial motivation are basically to render labour more productive and void of corruption. But in Cameroon such high financial motivations are there to encourage individuals to accept and sustain a system of governance which has failed in satisfying the aspirations of the Cameroon population over a relatively long period.

In Cameroon most persons identify with the ruling party (party in power) not because of any ideology it represents, not because of any good results it has obtained, but because it does not only offer you a passport to unbridled riches but also shields you from criminal persecution. You want to obtain

[1] Meaning the appointed persons are entitled to advantages of all sorts made available by the regulation in place.

funds for a contract and go scot free without executing the contract- join the ruling party. You want to be considered for plum jobs without the appropriate profile - join the ruling party and so on. And as soon as such persons join the party they do all in their power to frustrate any attempts to redress some of the crucial problems plaguing the country.

iv). Corruption, Embezzlement and Misappropriation of State Resources

Despite the numerous facilities and opportunities put at the disposal of our top government officials, their propensity to get more persists. Most of them embezzle, misappropriate, and devise all sorts of strategies necessary to divert money from the state coffers into their pockets. This seems to be the main occupation of state officials in Cameroon. Today, some of these personalities have been arrested and sent to prison on corruption charges, but the comportment of those still in service has not changed, and there is thus evidence that those in service today may likely be in prison tomorrow.

Cameroon has been operating with impunity a system of institutionalized corruption for decades. This corruption stems from state institutions and spreads to all the sectors of our economy. The powers that be know that such practices do exist, but nothing draconian has been done to put an end to them. We have been hearing of huge sums of money given as bribe to gain admission into our professional institutions (ENAM, ENS, CUSS, ESSTIC etc). We have been hearing of the payment of some sums representing some percentages to authorities (DOs, Mayors, Governors, Ministers) before public projects are executed anywhere in Cameroon. We have been hearing of payment of bribes (*gombo*) to civil servants, especially in the Finance and Public Service Ministries before files are treated, and so on. State authorities know about all such allegations, but since they are effective beneficiaries of the system they do not care.

The arrests and imprisonment of corrupt officers in Cameroon do not in any way deter other officials from indulging in the practice. It is like the gene of corruption has been carefully injected into the blood of Cameroonians. But who could have injected such a gene into our blood streams?

The fight against corruption in Cameroon has been simplified to arrests and imprisonment of some persons charged with corruption. This could be compared to a situation where attempts are being made to fill water in a bucket with a hole under through which the water leaks out permanently. Thus in reality, the fight against corruption in Cameroon has not yet begun. Until the problems of impunity, favoritism, laxity, nepotism, tribalism and other societal ills are adequately addressed in Cameroon, the war against corruption will be getting more and more difficult and complicated as days go by. Consequently, Cameroon will continue to pay the high price imposed by this *"come no go"*.

v). Investment Expenditure - Far from being a Priority

The Cameroon 2012 budget was to be implemented against the backdrop of the presidential declaration that Cameroon would be transformed into a huge construction site (Grandes Realizations) commencing January of the same year. The translation into reality of this dream should be directly contingent on huge investment and favourable conditions for doing business in Cameroon. The annual rates of investment in Cameroon have been relatively very low for decades. Such rates cannot generate the economic growth needed to sustain the Cameroon economy. For more than two decades, Cameroon's annual growth rates have been confined in the bracket (2%-5%), giving an average of about 3% over the period. This growth rate is not sustainable because it is not significantly different from the population growth rate (2.6%).

Cameroon requires a minimum sustained annual growth rate of 7.5% before Cameroonians could start feeling a positive change from the hardship experienced for more than three decades. This rate can be registered and sustained only if some fundamental positive changes occurred in the economic management system in Cameroon as well as in good governance. It is only from such a sustained level of growth (7.5%), which must increase in the course of time that we are capable of estimating the emerging year for the economy of Cameroon. When the present government is talking about the emergence of the Cameroon economy in 2035, they are basing their judgment more on simulation exercises or assumptions which are not backed by any empirical evidence. It is not very different from signing a decree for that purpose.

vi). State Resources Squandered at all Levels

Human beings are said to be unfortunate because they are plagued with unlimited wants which compel them to economize the limited resources needed to satisfy these wants. Cameroonians appear to be special human beings as they squander resources as if they were as unlimited as the wants. The Cameroon public sector is characterized by some high degree of waste at all levels. With respect to the state budget, a reasonable portion of the budget spending goes into ceremonial activities (seminars, ghost missions, entertainment etc.). Seminars are often organized for just any possible thing. Cameroon is one place where a seminar would be organized to conceive a project, another is organized to study the feasibility of the project, another to train people to execute the project and yet another to put the project in place. The ultimate goal of such seminars is to snatch money from the state treasury. It is institutionalized corruption, i.e. corruption in its most official form.

In connection with the 2012 budget, Honourable Ayah Paul Abine, a member of parliament, demonstrated with figures how Cameroon's State budget has been an instrument of underdevelopment and waste for decades. Hon. Ayah highlighted some headings like entertainment and common expenditure which carry huge sums of money every year without any information on how such monies are spent. He highlighted that in an economy like ours, it is totally inadmissible for the Secretary General of the Presidency, for example, to be allocated 2.5million per day for fuel in the state budget.

It is common knowledge that for the 2012 budget, entertainment stood at 57 billions and common expenditure at 28 billions giving a total of 85 billion francs. This amount either takes care of futile issues or gets directly into people's pockets. This wasted amount (85 billion francs) could be used to construct and equip several hospitals and schools in Cameroon, only for the year 2012. In addition to this, the government of Cameroon spends billions of francs each month to pay salaries of ghost workers. The phenomenon of ghost workers has existed in the Cameroon public service for decades. The corrupt nature of the public service facilitates the presence of ghost workers. It is estimated that there could be about 40 000 ghost workers in the country who take home a sum of about 5 billion francs every month as salaries. Is this an exaggeration?

Imagine what Cameroon could have been if these amounts were used every year for productive purposes in the last 52 years. This probably explains why countries like China and South Korea that were worse off than Cameroon in the 70s are today highly developed countries which we turn to for aid.

4. Conclusion

The problems hindering the emergence of Cameroon are known, and some are highlighted above. When you know the cause of an ailment, and are determined to solve the problem, you are certainly on the path of success. Cameroon has been and continues to be one of the most qualified candidates in Africa for economic emergence yet it remains the laughing stock of the continent. Moreover, it has within it all the momentum needed for that purpose, and can join the wagon of emerging nations in about ten years from today if the minimum requirements are made. What has been lacking, and is still lacking is a resolute vision and action focused in that direction. The essential rituals have not been performed, and we are not yet positioned in the track that can lead to emergence. The talk about the emergence of Cameroon in 2035 seems to me a slogan, carefully tailored to blindfold the public and set the politicians free from the present messy situations.

The Cameroon economy is not yet independent, and our leaders appear to be comfortable in that situation. The colonial masters are still present in various forms, and continue to amass most of our resources for their economies. The present Cameroon leadership is not yet focused on issues that can carry the nation forward. Most state issues of interest are attributed political overtones which most of the time end up in the interests of politicians. For a given amount of state resources, the interests of the state are often in keen competition with the personal interests of those called upon to manage such resources, and most of the time such personal interests tend to predominate. Could it be that those responsible for taking Cameroon to emergence are yet to emerge?

It is in the light of all these that I heartily welcome this book ***Cameroon a Lion deeply asleep: Building a new***

Cameroon by Rev. Fr. Linus Patem. I do strongly believe that any Cameroonian who loves this country will take time to read and meditate on it. And truly, if all leaders and citizens of this country were to show their patriotism by trying to earnestly put into practice what Father has to say in this book, it will not take long before this nation and its people begin to experience real growth and prosperity. This, indeed, is my prayer and hope.

NSOM JOSEPH

Economist and Statistician

MINISTRY OF ECONOMY, PLANNING AND REGIONAL DEVELOPMENT, YAOUNDÉ

PART ONE

BUILDING GOOD GOVERNANCE

INTRODUCTION TO PART ONE

What Cameroon really stands in dire need of in order to attain the growth and prosperity that constitutes the greatest aspiration of its people is good governance. According to the United Nations Economic and Social Commission for Asia and the Pacific (UNESCAP), good governance has eight key characteristics:

> *It is participatory, consensus oriented, accountable, transparent, responsive, effective and efficient, equitable and inclusive and follows the rule of law. It assures that corruption is minimized, the views of minorities are taken into account and that the voices of the most vulnerable in society are heard in decision-making. It is also responsive to the present and future needs of society*[2].

FIGURE 2: *Characteristics of good governance*

---

[2] http://www.unescap.org/pdd/prs/ProjectActivities/Ongoing/gg/governance.asp

Once a government exhibits the qualities cited above, it is evident that the nation concerned is experiencing good governance. It is widely admitted that the worst crisis that has been wrecking our nation since independence, as it is the case with the rest of Africa, is bad governance. This explains why, in spite of the abundance of natural and human resources with which God has blessed this country, it has not been able to extricate itself from the grip of poverty.

Were Africa to be blessed with real statesmen and women as leaders who are capable of promoting good governance, it would, in no time, be transformed into a paradise on earth. But who is supposed to be at the forefront of building this sort of government that our countries in Africa so badly need? It is the ordinary citizens who paradoxically usually prove to be naïve, complacent, indolent and ignorant.

This book is certainly addressed to all Cameroonians irrespective of their faith and background. As citizens of this nation, we all have equal rights and responsibilities towards the welfare of our nation and its people. But I have decided to address the issue of good governance in the opening chapters, in the first place, to Christians and not without reason. They have received from Christ the mandate to be leaders after his own example and not to emulate leaders who govern according to the standards of this world:

> *You know that the rulers of the Gentiles lord it over them, and the great ones make their authority over them felt. But it shall not be so among you. Rather, whoever wishes to be great among you shall be your servant; whoever wishes to be first among you shall be your slave. Just so, the son of Man did not come to be served but to serve and to give his life as a ransom for many*[3].

[3]Matthew 20:25-28.

And what is more, he has commissioned his disciples to be the foundation on which good governance, development and prosperity are to be built in a nation: *"you are the salt of the earth...you are the light of the world"*[4].

It follows therefore that even if Christians formed only a small part of those who serve in the government of our country, their impact would nevertheless have constituted a form of catalyst that would have irresistibly transformed our society for the better. But we know that the reverse is true. They constitute the bulk of those who occupy top leadership positions of one kind or the other in the government of our nation but unfortunately less performant. Cameroon therefore, finds itself in a terrible state of socio-political and economic paralysis. The conclusion is easy to draw: not enough effort has been made to carry out the mission Christ has given us his followers, namely to be the *salt* and *light* of the world, and to seek leadership positions for the sole purpose of serving others and not in order to be served.

The men and women, who hold leadership positions in our government, certainly ought to be aware that the authority they possess in their respective offices comes from none other than God. God's own word is clear about this, "*(...) there is no authority except from God, and those that exist have been established by God*"[5]. If others possess and use this authority without recognizing its source, it must not be so with our Christian leaders. They are supposed to be conscious of this truth that everything they do in government ought to be enlightened and guided by the faith they profess in Christ, whose disciples they are. In fact, our leaders in government, like all other Christian citizens, are called to live a life of perfection in whatever state of life or function which they occupy. This is the admonishment that Our Lord Jesus has

[4]Matthew 5: 13-14.
[5] Romans 13: 1.

given to his followers: "*So be perfect just as your heavenly Father is perfect*"[6]. And the Second Vatican Council in its Decree on the Church in the Modern World, *Lumen Gentium* reiterated the same teaching:

> *The faithful of Christ of whatever rank or status are called to the fullness of the Christian life and to the perfection of charity. By this holiness a more human way of life is promoted even in this earthly society*[7].

This teaching of the Council was put even more succinctly by Pope John Paul I when drawing attention to the great importance of the mission of Opus Dei to the Church and society today:

> *Christ does not want us simply to be good; he wants us to be saints through and through. However, he wants us to attain that sanctity not by doing extraordinary things, but rather, through ordinary common activities. It is the way that they are done which must be uncommon"...in the middle of the street, in the office, in the factory, we can be holy provided we do our job competently, for love of God, and cheerfully, so that everyday work does not become 'a daily tragedy', but rather 'a daily smile'*[8].

It therefore follows that unless a Christian leader is holy, he or she cannot contribute in any substantial way to the attainment of real peace and prosperity for their country. In this light, Pope John Paul I This is why the Special Assembly for Africa of the Synod of Bishops fervently prayed that,

> *There would arise in Africa holy politicians – both men and women and that there would be saintly*

---

[6] Matthew 5: 48.

[7] *Lumen Gentium*, no. 40.

[8] Pope John Paul I, in *Il Gazzettino*, (Venice: July, 1978).

Heads of state, who profoundly love their own people and wish to serve rather than be served[9].

But a fundamental question may be posed at this point: how does God expect leaders to use the authority he has given them in serving the people he has placed under their charge? I find the answer contained in the following admonition given by the Lord himself to the leaders of nations in the Book of Wisdom:

*Hear, therefore, kings, and understand; learn, you magistrates of the earth's expanse! Give ear, you who have power over multitudes and lord it over throngs of peoples! Because authority was given you by the Lord and sovereignty by the Most High, who shall probe your works and scrutinize your counsels! Because, though you were ministers of his kingdom, you did not judge rightly **(govern justly)**, and did not keep the law **(uphold the law)**, nor **walk according to the will of God**, Terribly and swiftly he shall come against you, because severe judgment awaits the exalted – For the lowly may be pardoned out of mercy but the mighty shall be mightily put to the test. For the Ruler of all shows no partiality, nor does he fear greatness, Because he himself made the great as well as the small, and provides for all alike; but for those in power a rigorous scrutiny impends. To you, therefore, O princes, are my words addressed that you may learn wisdom and that you may not fall away. For those who keep the holy precepts hallowed will be found holy, and those learned in them will have ready a response. Desire therefore*

[9] John Paul II, *Ecclesia in Africa*, no. 111, (Yaoundé: 14 September, 1995).

my words; long for them and you will be instructed[10]. (Emphasis mine)

This passage of Sacred Scripture does bring out the three principal duties of those in authority on whose fulfillment good governance depends. These are:

- **to govern justly**
- **to uphold the law and**
- **to live according to the will of God**

And the basic reason for which they must use their power and authority in this way is because, as the Lord himself declares, that they ministers of his kingdom[11].

There is no doubt that there are at least a few in our government who are doing their best to avoid all unclean practices, but even these are under the constant temptation to follow the majority who do not allow their faith to guide them in the way they handle public office. However, we must constantly remind ourselves that when it comes to the service of God and our nation, what matters is not following the crowd who may be behaving recklessly but conscientiously striving to do what we are convinced is right and just. In the words of Oscar Luigi Salfaro, former President of Italy, this is really what is of interest, for, as he observes:

The Lord will not judge a people, but persons individually. And I will not be able to say: 'As no one got involved, I didn't get involved either'. What is important for the Lord is if I did my duty[12].

The following chapters of the first part of this book constitute a brief consideration of how state authorities are to

---

[10] Wisdom 6: 1-11.

[11] Cf. Wisdom 6:4.

[12]NN, *Ex-Italian President Salfaro on the Lack of Christian Politicians* , in Zenith, (May 23, 2003), p. 1.

carry out the three-fold responsibilities enjoined by the Lord. My hope in presenting all these is to help the present and future leaders of this country to better understand what good governance is all about and what needs to be done to steer Cameroon out of its present state of stupor into real development and prosperity. If these reminders serve to firmly implant good governance and its accompanying fruits in all the strata of our government and society, I shall have accomplished my aim.

Fr. Linus PATEM

CHAPTER 1

GOVERNING JUSTLY

GOD has given power to state authorities so that they may govern His people according to His will. He therefore, requires that they should carry out this stupendous exercise justly, for this is exactly how He himself governs creation. Justice is clearly one of the three chief attributes of God, and those in authority cannot please Him except they act justly in all they do in the exercise of their office.

Unfortunately, most of our Christian brothers and sisters in leadership positions in our government seem to have little concern about justice and fair play in governance. This means they have failed in the fulfillment of one of the key responsibilities of their God-given talent. It is thus expected that for Christ's sake and for the good of our country, they should either immediately amend or resign from their respective offices. Without just governance any hope of achieving any real development in Cameroon or building a better and prosperous nation will be nothing but a delusion.

Now, what does just governance demand of our state authorities?

i. It demands of whoever aspires to the office of the President of the Republic that he accepts the office of Head of State only if he is certain that he or she has the majority votes as stipulated by the constitution in a free and fair election. And should one have any fears that there were some irregularities or unjust practices in the process of the election, he or she must not accept the office of president. This applies equally to Members of Parliament and heads of Municipal governments who accede to their offices or authority through democratic elections.

ii. It demands of our Parliamentarians that they should not prioritize personal or party interest when elaborating laws that govern the country. Parliamentarians are supposed to focus their attention on the welfare of Cameroonians and the glory of God. This means that they should never twist the constitution to suit their personal ambitions or that of the Head of State. State authorities or government officials who seek to have the constitution reworked to accommodate their personal interests can be likened to unjust and corrupt business individuals who use false measures like tampering with the scales with the intention of cheating their customers thus maximizing their profits at the expense of others. Concerning persons who practice such injustices, the Lord says: *"The Lord has sworn by the pride of Jacob: Never will I forget a thing they have done! ... I will turn your feasts into mourning and all your songs into dirges."*[13]

iii. Governing justly demands that state authorities who have the power to make appointments choose only the most trustworthy and dependable men and women to serve in our government at all levels. It equally obliges that those who act or behave in a manner unworthy of the office entrusted to them, or who misuse their office in any way whatsoever, or who in one way or the other prove to be incompetent, should be immediately relieved of their duties, and suitable persons appointed to replace them. The principle of justice, as far as appointments to government positions is concerned, is always to have a square peg in a square hole, that is – the right person in the right office or position. Corrupt persons or

[13] Amos 8:8, 10.

embezzlers, whose aspiration is to enrich themselves from the public coffers or nation's wealth, as well as all those who place personal interest over the common good, certainly should have no place in our government.

iv. Just governance obliges that those whose duty it is to designate people to positions of authority should never base their choice on tribal, party or family considerations or on other unworthy motives, but strictly on competence or aptitude. Complains abound of certain tribal groups dominating in government and other national institutions due to unjust practices which favour one class to the detriment of others. This situation breeds national animosity and lays the bases for civic strife.

v. To govern justly requires that no state authority ever accepts or demands a bribe or gift in exchange for a position in government. Such action itself involves a double crime before God: *injustice* and *theft*, which are without doubt very grave. Thieves, as Scripture teaches, shall not inherit the Kingdom of God[14].

vi. Just governance also means that no political party, whether a ruling or non-ruling one, should hijack and misappropriate public funds in anyway whatsoever. It further demands that no individual in authority should ever abuse his God-given authority by taking for his own use money or resources that are meant for the common good. Apart from the serious crime involved, it is quite a shameful thing for a Christian occupying a public office to enrich himself or swell his bank account with the nation's wealth or treat public funds or property as if they belong to him personally. There are countless numbers of such people in this country who are milking state coffers dry and are growing terribly rich through all

---

[14] Cf. 1 Cor. 6: 10.

kinds of corrupt and fraudulent practices. This is a situation which the Bishops of Cameroon have always decried. In their Pastoral Letter on Corruption published some years ago they wrote inter alia:

> *Fraud, cheating, sexual and financial harassment, have been turned into universal principles and kill the values of truth, justice, and transparency, often wrongly regarded as the virtues of the weak. This situation is very serious for the formation of our young people, for the quality of our teaching and for the future of our country in general*[15].

Christians who have abandoned their calling and used their authority to cheat and steal what belongs to the people in order to greedily amass wealth for themselves, need to pay heed to these words of St. James:

> *Come now, you rich, weep and wail over your impending miseries. Your wealth has rotted away, your clothes have become moth-eaten, your gold and silver have corroded, and that corrosion will be a testimony against you; it will devour your flesh like a fire*[16].

For these persons to repent of their crimes and be reconciled with God and their country, it is certainly not enough for them to refrain from swindling the nation's resources. Neither is it enough for them to be put in jail. More than this, they must make full restitution of what they have stolen or fraudulently made use of. In fact, justice obliges all who have in one way or another robbed this country of whatever belongs to its people to make full

---

[15] The National Episcopal Conference of Cameroon (NECC), *Pastoral Letter on Corruption*, no. 42, (Bamenda, 2000).
[16] James 5: 2-3.

restitution and, in the case of stolen money, to put back the full sum embezzled into the nation's treasury.

The Fathers of the Special Assembly of the Synod of Bishops for Africa drew attention in a strong way to the need for restitution: *"We appeal to all our African brothers who have embezzled public funds that they are bound in justice to redress the wrong done to our peoples"*. In this light, the Bishops of Cameroon further noted:

> *What is true of public funds is evidently valid also for private societies, the Church and wrongs committed against persons. What I have stolen through corrupt means, or taken by trickery or threat does not belong to me and it must be returned to its rightful owner*[17].

According to the Catechism of the Catholic Church, *"Reparation for injustice committed requires the restitution of stolen goods to their owner"*[18]. Repentance and restitution are always necessary for the reparation of the sin of theft or injustice.

On the part of the government, it must ensure that those who in any way have been or are involved in corruption or embezzlement (which has so lamentably paralyzed our country economically) should be brought to justice according to the laws of the land. Such is the request of the Bishops of Cameroon, who have observed that the lack of justice is the principal reason for the rapid growth of corruption in our country:

> *Impunity is certainly the main reason for the rapid advance of corruption in our country. We ask once more and with insistence, that those involved in corruption and the theft of public funds be brought*

---

[17] John Paul II, Ecclesia in Africa, no. 37, (Yaoundé, 1995).
[18] *The Catechism of the Catholic Church,* no. 2412.

before the courts and judged according to the law, so that our country might finally begin to live in peace and security[19].

i. Good governance further obliges state authorities to see into it that neither they nor any other citizen twists the course of justice and that no one ever violates the rights of the people. Whoever does so is abominable to the Lord who has warned: "*Woe to those who turn justice into wormwood and cast righteousness to the ground...*"[20] Surely, there is a breach of justice when, as it is so rampant in our courts of law, the Magistrate or the Judge acquits the guilty and declares the innocent guilty either because he has been bribed or because of some other evil motives. There is a serious violation of the rights of the people and a breach of justice when the property of citizens is destroyed without appropriate compensation or their houses are demolished without their families having been relocated. Those who have carried out or assisted in these unchristian and inhuman acts know that justice obliges them to fully compensate all whom they have deprived of their property. Justice delayed is justice denied. Many are those who are languishing in detention camps in this country without even as much as a charge levied against them. Just governance does not tolerate this kind of situation. In this regard, Pope Benedict XVI in his Post-Synodal Apostolic Exhortation *Africae Munus* on the Church in Africa in service of Reconciliation, Justice and Peace, admonishes:

"It is time to put a stop to "miscarriages of justice... which represent a violation of human rights," as

---

[19]NECC., *Pastoral Letter on Corruption*, no. 44, (Bamenda, 2000).
[20] Amos 5: 7.

well as imprisonment either without trial or else with much-delayed trial.[21] "

We have to overhaul inefficient systems and engage friendly legal systems that offer justice to all persons without prejudice.

ii. Good governance obliges all employers, especially state officials responsible for paying government employees to ensure that their employees receive their salaries promptly at the stipulated time and that these salaries are commensurate to the work they do for the state. This also means that people should not have to go to Yaoundé from other parts of the country to "follow up" their wages before they receive them. It is clearly unjust and displeasing to God to have poor countrymen and women abandon their families alone for days, weeks and sometimes months, and subject themselves to all sorts of risks in order to run after what is rightfully theirs. Technology and better software for managing state personnel have been put in place and these can be used to ensure that employees can receive their dues at their doorsteps. Besides, who pays for the time and money wasted in the process of 'chasing papers or dossiers' from one place to another? Who compensates for the stress that these poor citizens and their families are subjected to? It is unfortunate to note that Cameroonians beg to be employed and beg to be paid and when they retire, they continue to bribe in order to be given that for which they had sweated to save for the rainy days of retirement.

I really cannot understand how a Christian can bear the sight of so many old, weak and poor retired citizens who every now and then are compelled to make long and tiring

[21]POPE BENEDICT XVI, Post-Synodal Apostolic Exhortation *Africae Munus,* (19 November, 2011), no. 82.

journeys, sometimes abandoning their sick beds, and waiting for days or weeks unend in order to collect their pensions from the Ministry of Finance or from the National Social Insurance offices which are located far away from their homes. Quite often those of them who succeed in having a few francs dropped into their hands, as if out of sheer charity, receive such a favour not only after having had many insults heaped on them but after exercising the most heroic patience. What is more painful, often these poor men and women can only hope to receive what they are due after having accepted to let go, to the payer's benefit, some percentage of the little sum they and their families depend on for livelihood. Who does not know that very often these old people – many of whom are widows and widowers – even after collecting a meager sum of money spend almost all they have received on food, transportation, medicine and lodging and sometimes return home with hardly enough money to pay their debts!

Sacred Scripture has made it plain that it is quite unjust and offending before God to withhold or delay the wages of employees: "*Woe to him... who works his neighbours without pay, and gives them no wages.*"[22] And concerning the wages of the poor in particular, the Lord addresses the following words to those who must pay them:

> *You shall not exploit a poor and needy hired servant ... On each day you shall pay the servant's wages before the sun goes down, since the servant is poor and is counting on them. Otherwise the servant will cry to the Lord against you, and you will be held guilty.*[23]

And St. James warns:

[22] Jeremiah 22: 13.
[23] Deut. 24: 14-15.

Behold the wages you withheld from the workers who harvested your fields are crying aloud, and the cries of the harvesters have reached the ears of the Lord of hosts.[24]

iii. Just governance demands that state authorities provide the necessary means and opportunities for all citizens to acquire the requisite training in life – be it temporal or religious to which the person considers himself or herself called. It also demands that they give the citizens, especially the young people, the help and encouragement they need to discover, develop and exercise their God-given talents both for their personal wellbeing and that of the nation.

iv. Governing justly obliges the government authorities concerned to ensure that young Cameroonians can acquire in their own country that sound education which is truly a preparation for a life of work and a meaningful living, each according to his or her aptitude. Presently, the custom is that if Cameroonians desire quality and meaningful education and the means of earning a decent livelihood, they have to look out of the country for these. And for this reason, a good number of our young people (the greatest human resource we have) are leaving the country. But this only means that we have failed to meet our obligations towards the young whose future is the future of this beloved nation given us by God. In our case it may well be said: "... *Children beg for bread, but no-one gives them a piece*"[25]. I have to say that I do not know what account many of us will have to render to God for our offices or positions if we do not immediately correct our short-comings and labour tirelessly as we ought to provide the youths of our nation with the

---

[24] James 5: 4.

[25] Cf. Lamentation 4: 4.

adequate means they need to build up and exercise their God-given potential and to fulfill their duties towards God and their country.

v. Furthermore, just governance ensures an equitable distribution of the wealth and resources of our nation to all the parts of the country in order to guarantee balanced development. State authorities to whom this wealth of the nation is entrusted are obliged in conscience to avoid concentrating all development efforts in some selected parts or areas of our nation while neglecting others. It certainly is a serious breach of justice on their part if they collect taxes and other levies from citizens in all parts of the country (or receive loans or donations in the name of all Cameroonians) but spend the money so received in the development of a few favoured areas or for the enhancement of the well-being of a selected few.

When one looks at the acute suffering or misery that countless Cameroonians in some parts of our country are going through and the lamentable state of underdevelopment that many parts of this country are in, it is evident that most of us have either not taken note of their situation or that such citizens or areas have no place in our hearts. It is certainly unchristian and even inhuman for leaders to treat their citizens with partiality. Some are living in affluence or even luxury while many are deprived even of the basic necessities of life: no access to good potable water or housing for their families, no access to basic health facilities, no good roads, no schools or (even when they are made available) they lack well-trained teachers and the necessary amenities to function properly and help those on whom the future of our beloved nation depends.

I have to confess that I do not know how we can live with peaceful consciences before God and our fellow compatriots if we do not, each according to his or her means and position, correct these lamentable injustices without delay and labour as we ought to alleviate the misery of our peoples and bring about a truly balanced development of our nation. We do not need the pressure that comes from the requirement to meet the Millennium Development Goals set for us by the international community in order to effectively embark on socio-economic and political development of our country.

FIGURE 3: *Improving the housing and living conditions of poor families in disadvantaged communities remains one of the principal tasks of government.*

The sorry state of our economy is a scandal to the intellectual cream that governs this country. By the same token, the governing elite and those loitering on the corridors of power all over the country are so obsessed with greed and occultism that they consider their Christian obligations as immaterial. Most fickle-minded Cameroonians have lost hope in our government leaders and the fragmented opposition leaders who see nothing wrong in the system but rather support it for the short-term material benefits while the country daily goes down the drain. In this regard, we would like to borrow from Scriptures to ask, *"What profit is there for a man to gain the whole world and forfeit his life?"*[26].

[26] Mark 8:37.

CHAPTER 2

UPHOLDING THE LAW

Concerning the observance of the law, our Lord declares: *"...whoever obeys and teaches these commandments will be called greatest in the kingdom of heaven"*[27]. Now, just as Christ used the authority he had received from his Father, not only to act and lead justly but also to *uphold the Law*,[28] so too must his disciples who share in his authority. Apart from governing justly, upholding the law is one of the reasons why God has granted his authority to leaders. The chief responsibility of those in government is to ensure that the law is respected. Where there is equity there is no iniquity. The growth of our country depends principally on the careful observance of the rule of law. In the words of the Synod of Bishops for Africa, "*The foundation of good government must be established on the sound basis of laws which protect the rights and define the obligations of the citizens*"[29]. And according to Pope Benedict XVI, *"the widespread non-enforcement of the law ...represents a violation of human rights.*[30]*"*

All laws, if they are good and just, come from God since he is the Supreme lawgiver. It is from him alone that all good things come. According to the teachings of our Lord, it is clear that those who disobey the law and teach others to do same will be the least in the kingdom of heaven, while the

---

[27]Matthew 5: 19.
[28]Cf. Matthew 5:17.
[29] John Paul II, *Ecclesia in Africa*, n° 112, (Yaoundé: 14 September, 1995).
[30]POPE BENEDICT XVI, Post-Synodal Apostolic Exhortation *Africae Munus,* (19 November, 2011), no. 82.

ones who obey the law and teach others to do same shall be great in the kingdom of heaven[31].

But, it is not possible for there to be the rule of law in our country unless a sound justice system has been put in place. The Bishops of Cameroon have observed with much pain that, whereas the mission of our judicial system is the triumph of justice and fair-play, the most serious forms of corruption in our country are to be found in this sector. They give a graphic description of the situation as follows:

> *Magistrates, judges and state counsels sell their judgment to the highest bidder. Detainees who cannot pay can spend years in prison, sometimes without ever having been brought before a court of law, and in flagrant violation of the human rights of people and the laws of the land. Even after the courts have given a verdict, its execution can take years. The poor and those who don't have 'someone' are becoming increasingly frightened of our court houses when they seek justice. Since they are excluded from the corruption network they are exposed to all kinds of injustices. The situation is particularly agonizing for those who are innocent of the accusations brought against them. Public and para-statal societies overcharge users for the services rendered. This situation is aggravated by the deficiencies of our judicial system which does not enable the victims of such actions to reclaim their rights*[32].

It is for this reason that the same Bishops strongly request as follows:

---

[31] Cf. Matthew 5: 19.

[32]NECC, *Pastoral Letter on the Economic Crisis*, (Yaoundé: June 3, 1990),no. 15.

We want a justice system that is upright and independent. We ask the government to take very great care of the moral integrity of those who administer justice and to let justice be done without interference[33].

Let us now consider how our state authorities in this country are required by God to use their authority to observe the law, which, as has been observed, constitutes one of their principal responsibilities with regard to establishing good governance.

i. Upholding the law means that our lawmakers such as the Parliamentarians and Senators should ensure that no laws are passed which compromise in any way whatsoever the laws of God. As earlier pointed out, God is the First and Supreme law-giver and has given laws for the sake of man's temporal and eternal well-being. Hence, no law which in anyway contradicts God's law can be of any good to man. Thus laws that, for example, promote or allow abortion, mercy-killing or the use of artificial birth control methods (contraceptives) and same-sex marriage clearly do not square with God's Laws, which are always aimed at protecting human life and not attacking or destroying it. Such laws would, without doubt, be detrimental to the wellbeing of our citizens. In fact, Christian parliamentarians need to always ask themselves this fundamental question whenever any bill is tabled for discussion and adoption: what would Jesus do if he were in my place? Would he support this bill or oppose it? In such circumstances, the will of God should overshadow all human interests, in imitation of Christ who always had as his guide in every decision the will of the one who sent him.[34]

---

[33] *Ibid.*, no. 45.

[34] Cf. John 4:34.

ii. Upholding the principle of the law means further that laws are not passed to benefit any political party or particular person or group of people but rather to foster the good and wellbeing of every Cameroonian. Similarly, the balance of power that must exist in every democracy obliges the legislative arm of our government (i.e. Parliamentarians and Senators) as well as the judiciary to stand out and be counted. They are not to be the stooges of the executive. They are not to work according to its dictates or its whims and caprices. All that need concern them, if they are really to fulfill their God-given duties, is to pass laws that will truly foster justice, peace and the balanced socio-economic and political growth of Cameroon. Thus if there are presently any laws that impede our country from arriving at these goals, the honourable members of Parliament are bound in conscience to ensure that they are abrogated.

iii. Upholding the law demands that our leaders should use their God-given power and all the means at their disposal to curb the present widespread violation of human rights and corruption in all their forms. In this country the bribery and corruption, which have already wrecked our country so badly, impoverishing the lives of millions of Cameroonians and the rampant human rights abuses (sometimes orchestrated by state officials) are fanned daily and or promoted by the non-enforcement of the laws prohibiting such criminal practices. In one of their pastoral letters, the Bishops of Cameroon, lamenting the high prevalence of human rights violations in our country, observed:

Living in the midst of the people God has entrusted to us, we cannot help but notice around us day in day out, violation evermore flagrant of the rights of human beings. The poor, the weak, the defenseless are subjected to the arbitrariness of unscrupulous civil servants, of the agents of the Law and order or even of persons of undefined positions acting under the cloak of the party or protected by some mysterious impunity which gives rise to scandal. Respectable citizens are struck down on our streets, loathsome crimes are covered up, followed by the silence of the apparent powerlessness of those to whom the people have entrusted their protection, the defense of their destiny, their goods and their lives[35].

These are precisely the evils that state authorities have been given power by God to prevent, and they are bound in conscience to do this and correct any past negligence in this regard. It is the Bishops' earnest appeal that they "*Ensure that our people in their present disarray should feel secure and experience, everywhere and at all times, the support and protection of the state*"[36].

iv. In addition, upholding the law requires not only those who make our laws but also those who implement them, namely our law courts, to be men and women of integrity and true custodians of the law. The office they hold is a very important and delicate one since there cannot be real justice, peace and prosperity in our country unless the law is judiciously upheld. Obviously, these constitute both the foundation and fruits of good governance. What is more, God will surely demand an account of them for failure to uphold the law, for this breeds nothing but crime and misery, which they have as their principal duty to prevent. Lawmakers have a duty to pass good laws and laws enforcers are supposed to uphold good laws and denounce bad ones. Normally, good laws are laws that are capable of fostering real freedom, peace and

---

[35] NECC, *Pastoral Letter on the Economic Crisis*, no. 15, (Yaoundé: June 3, 1990).
[36] *Ibid.*

prosperity for the citizens. The Lord's admonition to corrupt and unjust lawmakers and judges shows the seriousness of this duty:

> *You are doomed! You make unjust laws that oppress my people. That is how you prevent the poor from having their rights and from getting justice. That is how you take the property that belongs to widows and orphans. What will you do when God punishes you?*[37]

It is perplexing when one observes that there are so many vulnerable Cameroonians who, because of their low standing in society, have had either their money or some other property due them withheld or even confiscated, sometimes even by people in authority. So many poor people, widows and orphans are being deprived of their rights and even trampled upon everyday by those with money and influence and it does not seem to bother them. But our good God has declared Himself a defender of the rights of the helpless[38]. Those who are willing to obtain His mercy need to correct all these injustices, and strive constantly to govern those under their charge with justice and integrity as the Lord Himself requires of them[39]. They are to do this by establishing and tirelessly implementing laws that will truly promote or bring about justice and peace and balanced development in all the nooks and crannies of this our nation and in every aspect: social, moral, economic, political and educational.

---

[37] Isaiah 10: 1-3.
[38] Cf. Isaiah 11: 4.
[39] Cf. Isaiah 11: 5.

CHAPTER 3

LIVING ACCORDING TO GOD'S WILL

If the lives of state or government authorities are not according to God's will, they will certainly lead the nation astray. This is a situation which the Lord decries: *"Those who lead this people lead them astray, and those who are led are swallowed up"*[40]. Government leaders are required to give good example to those God has put in their care (the citizens). It is this message which the Bishops of Cameroon wished to pass across to our government leaders and politicians when they taught as follows:

> *C'est aussi à cause de sa fidélité à l'évangile que le chrétien doit s'engager dans la vie politique. La foi chrétienne n'est pas purement intérieure et privée : elle doit avoir des prolongements sociaux, économiques, politiques et culturels*[41].

Any nation stands or falls with its leaders. Generally speaking, people hardly rise above their leaders in virtue, since they are like the eyes of the body. If the eyes are sound, the whole body will be full of light; but if the eyes are not good, the body will be in darkness[42]. That is, if the leaders of a country live a life of integrity and moral rectitude as God

---

[40] Isaiah 9: 15.

[41] CEC, *Lettre Pastorale sur l'Engagement Des Laïcs dans la vie de la Nation,* (Ngoundéré : le 15 Janvier 1988), no.9: "It is by reason of their faithfulness to the Gospel that the Christian must take part in political activities. The faith of the Christian is not something which is only interior or private; it must extend to the social, economic, political and cultural life".

[42] Cf. Mt. 6: 22, 23.

requires, they will easily induce their citizens to live upright and will lead their nation to peace and prosperity. The same holds good for the parents of a family. However, if they live like people who have little or no regard for God and his Laws, then they will be the cause of immense misery and ruin for the people and nation.

For example, if those in authority are wont to steal from the public coffers as has often been reported in this country, or if they are prune to corrupt or dishonest practices in business, politics and government, the citizens will tend to become bolder in committing these monstrous crimes. And who needs to be told that this is the sort of calamity which has befallen this country of ours? There are even those Christians who attach more veracity and urgency to some government policy or party doctrine than the teaching of Christ and cling to them with greater tenacity sometimes to the point of self-immolation, even when such policies or doctrines are clearly incompatible with the will of God. Hence, if our state authorities are not God-fearing, and if they don't strive constantly to lead their country according to his will, they will certainly constitute an almost insurmountable obstacle to the growth of the nation and likewise the cause of the temporal and eternal ruin of many.

But which are some of the key ways in which Christians, especially those in leadership positions, are required to live according to God's holy will from day-to-day as they exercise the power of governance which has been entrusted to them?

i. They have to ensure that they do not use their offices or positions in government to enrich themselves dishonestly or fraudulently, for nothing seems to be more detestable to God than those who, though put in power to cater for the common good and wellbeing of the people, rather engage in growing rich at the expense of the citizens.

Instead of feeding the people entrusted to their care such persons deprive them of even the little means of livelihood they would have survived on. The truth which many Cameroonian Christians have not convinced themselves about is that money or property dishonestly acquired, far from being of any good or help to them and their families, builds for them nothing but a future of terrible misery and pain. St. James has given us a strong reminder of the dreadful future that those who accumulate riches through cheating, stealing or embezzlement are preparing for themselves through their corrupt and dishonest practices:

> *Come now, you rich, weep and wail over your impending miseries. Your wealth has rotted away... You have fattened your hearts for the day of slaughter*[43].

And our Bishops of Cameroon quoting the Prophet Amos add:

> *Hear this, you who trample upon the needy and destroy the poor of the land: 'When will the new moon be over' you ask, 'that we may sell our grain, and the Sabbath, that we open the grain-bins? We will diminish the ephah, add to the shekel, and fix our scales for cheating! We will buy the destitute for silver, and the poor for a pair of sandals; even the worthless grain we will sell!' The Lord has sworn by the pride of Jacob: never will I forget a thing they have done!*[44]

And if the rich man was condemned for simply failing or neglecting to feed the poor from his justly acquired resources or wealth, what will become of those in our country – so vast

---

[43] James 5: 1-3, 5.
[44] Amos 8: 4-7.

in number – who use government positions to deprive even the poor widow of her mite which is due her as pension for long years of service to her country? Some, though it is within their power and competence to pay poor labourers their wages – as meager as they often are – do not hesitate to cheat them even of the little that is due them and transfer same to their own bank accounts or perhaps withhold it for as long as it pleases them.

As for those who do not stop at cheating or stealing from individual citizens but go as far as diverting through misappropriation or embezzlement of state funds meant for national developmental accomplishments, I feel myself incapable of addressing them. Who will ponder about the monstrous guilt that they have or are accumulating before God without shuddering? Blessed John Paul II, in Post-Synodal Exhortation *Ecclesia in Africa*, notes with disappointment, as the Bishops of Cameroon recall, that many of Africa's problems, especially in the area of politics and economics,

> *Are the results of a manner of government often stained by corruption? A serious reawakening of conscience linked to a firm determination of will is necessary, in order to put into effect solutions which can no longer be put off*[45].

The Bishops, in the words of the Gospel, invite our state authorities to hearken to the will of God by putting an end to all forms of intimidation, extortion or corruption: they should be content with their pay[46]. In this regard, the Second Vatican council teaches:

> *It is by no means lawful therefore that citizens with abundant income derived from the resources and*

---

[45]John Paul II, *Ecclesia in Africa*, (Rome, 1994), no.110.
[46] Cf. NECC, *Pastoral Letter on Corruption*, no.13.

> *work of their native land transfer a large part of their income to foreign countries looking solely to their own private advantage, giving no consideration to their own country on which they inflict obvious harm by this conduct*[47].

And Pope Paul VI, summarizing the teaching of the Fathers of the Church on this matter pointed out that,

> "*The earth belongs to all, not to the rich*"[48]. And therefore, "*that the revenues derived from this source are not to be left to men's good pleasure and that plans for excessive profit made only for one's own advantage should be prohibited*"[49].

---

[47] *Gadium et Spes*, no. 65.
[48] Pope Paul VI, Encyclical Letter *Populorum Progressio*, n° 23, (Rome: March 26, 1967).
[49] *Ibid.*

CHAPTER 4

OUR CIVIL SERVANTS AND THEIR PRINCIPAL DUTIES

An appointment to serve our fatherland in a government position of any sort must be seen by a Christian as a real honour indeed. For, God Himself, when He deigned to become man chose no other state of life but that of a servant. And what is more, he bid his disciples to seek not positions of honour or authority, as pagans do, in order to lord it over others. Rather, they should rejoice in being servants to their brethren, for in this does true greatness consist[50].

It must be admitted that there are a number of our Christian men and women who having been honoured with positions in government, understand their appointments as a call to serve God and their fellow citizens. Thus they carry out the duties of their office after the example of Christ, our divine Master. Such persons do their work not just for earthly pay, that is the monthly salary, but above all to please God and to render a necessary service to their fellow citizens. They therefore have the good of our nation at heart and use their offices and positions for this end, knowing as they should that God will reward them for all they do. It can be said of these citizens what Jesus said to Nicodemus: they are civil servants and Christians worthy of the name, with nothing false in that[51]. Unfortunately, Cameroonians of this kind are, lamentably, so few and far below the margin to create the necessary impact.

---

[50] Cf. Mt. 20: 26-27.
[51] Cf. John 1: 47.

The bulk of the Christians who serve our nation in one government position or another seem to have accepted such places more for selfish motives than from the desire to serve God by serving their fellow countrymen. Some are so corrupt and dishonest that their proper place ought not to really be in public office but in a prison cell. They spend their time trying to satisfy nobody but their selfish ends. Their greatest desire is to fill their pockets with ill-gotten money and not to work for the good of Cameroon.

Others are either lazy or perhaps not well trained for their job or simply do not have any real interest in the work which they have been employed to do. This lack of interest is displayed in a variety of ways: habitual late coming to work, leaving the office before time, idling during working hours sometimes in drinking places, being rude and sarcastic towards those they are called upon to serve, and delays or reluctance to render services to the public. Yet at the end of the month, such corrupt or incompetent personnel also present themselves at the pay counter for a wage which they know that they do not deserve. Just like state authorities or employers who embezzle or unjustly withhold others' wages will have much to account for to God, so too will employees who, having not faithfully done their duties, collect a wage for what they have not done. All that such employees have collected in the name of salaries is nothing but stolen money, and they are bound in conscience to refund all that to the public treasury.

As it was indicated above, Christians who through appointments or some other just means occupy positions in our Civil Service ought to see themselves as called by God to serve him and their brothers and sisters as Christ did. If they understood the dignity that is attached to what they do, they would constantly be rejoicing for having been honoured with the same function that our Lord himself was pleased to perform in this world. They are to imitate him in their respective offices in the Public Service by serving as follows:

i. Avoiding any practice that opposes the Commandments of God or the Civil Code. For example, they should avoid allowing themselves to be corrupted by those who need their services or taking part in any other form of dishonesty, for all such evil conduct is contrary to their calling. It certainly cannot be denied that, as the Bishops have painfully noted, situations do abound in this country in which citizens find themselves under serious temptations to give bribe or act in some other corrupt way[52]. But as the same prelates point out, "*Those who refuse the corruption game in such circumstances accomplish an act of great nobility and do honour to our country*"[53]. Undoubtedly, to do so is always not easy but the Lord has not promised us that to be his disciples is always easy. On the contrary, he makes it clear that only those who are ready to suffer, if need be, for his sake can be his disciples, and that the only door that leads to eternal life is the narrow one[54].

ii. Patiently bearing any sacrifices associated with their offices or functions.

iii. Making judicious use of government or common property and resources and avoiding all forms of wastage especially of time.

iv. Giving the public the best of their services bearing in mind that the Lord takes as done to Himself whatever they do unto their fellow citizens, and that the growth of

---

[52]Cf. N.E.C.C., *Pastoral Letter on Corruption*, no. 10.
[53]Ibid.
[54] Cf. Matthew25: 40.

our nation and their salvation depend on the quality of their services[55].

v. Not yielding to any form of request to use their office or position in a way contrary to the precepts of the Gospel, preferring to suffer, if necessary, even unto death itself rather than offending God by abusing their offices. To this end, they need to constantly keep in mind these words of the Lord: "*Therefore do not be afraid of those who kill the body but cannot kill the soul; rather, be afraid of He who can kill both body and soul in Gehenna ...*"[56] And elsewhere he declares, "*For whoever wishes to save his life will lose it*"[57].

vi. Not letting themselves to be manipulated to misuse their office by any particular political party, even if it is the ruling party, since they are employed by the government to serve not the interest of a political party but public interests. And what is more, the money with which they are paid is from taxes which are paid by all Cameroonians and not just by members of a single party. Unfortunately, many Civil Servants have associated themselves with this act of injustice. This notwithstanding, Christians should take the lead in breaking with this unjust practice, which is so common in our country today among state employees who are using their offices to serve the interest of the ruling party. Should any party or anybody at all threaten them with punishment or dismissal if they refuse to bow to the party's wishes or interests, they must answer them with the words of the holy Apostles: "*We must obey God rather than men*"[58]. This, they should say in all sincerity

---

[55] Cf. Mt. 25: 40.
[56] Mt. 19: 28.
[57] Mk. 8: 35.
[58] Acts 5: 29.

since it is ultimately to the Lord they will have to give an account of their stewardship and not to fellow men. And should they be found then to have been wasteful or reckless in the exercise of their duties and misuse of the offices entrusted to them no earthly power or authority will be able to intervene on their behalf before God.

vii. Praying constantly for the grace of God to fulfill the duties entrusted to them with due diligence and faithfulness, for it is certain that without the Lord's special help, which comes especially through prayer, no one can persevere in doing good[59]. In Cameroon especially, where corruption and many other immoral practices are increasingly taken to be normal ways of life, how can a Christian citizen, particularly if he or she is serving in the Public Service – replete as it is with all kinds of temptations and scandals – obtain the light and fortitude to walk faithfully on the narrow and hard road which alone leads to life, if constant prayer is wanting?

[59] Cf. John 15: 5.

CHAPTER 5

OUR LAW ENFORCEMENT OFFICIALS AND DEFENCE PERSONNEL

What has been said about Christians in positions of authority and those in the Civil Service naturally applies also to our law enforcement and defense or military officers. Yet I think it necessary to say a few words specifically to these our brothers and sisters in uniform, because of the uniqueness of their vocation.

It is to be regretted that in this country many have the impression that the military or police services are for illiterates and people of low educational and moral standing. And in actual fact, we too often see these services filled by young men and women of very poor academic standing who seem to have no regard for basic moral values. Some of these do not even know their role as soldiers, which is to see to the safety of the citizens. The general tendency for many of them is to be barbaric, aggressive and immoral. It is common to see some of them manhandling and brutalizing or even attacking the very people whom they are called to defend or protect. How many innocent lives have been lost because of their recklessness or downright malice? How many people have suffered the loss of property through looting by them? How many have been disabled by our boys in uniform? A good number of them are not even educated about the rights of the citizen, and so often act in ways, which are incompatible with the welfare of the people. Many, indeed, are supposed to be in jail for using brute force and even arms on harmless civilians.

This is the dark side, but it does not take away the red feather from the hat of those among them, not small in numbers, who are serving this country and its people with love and dedication. They should continue to allow themselves to be guided by the example of that great military official whose faith was so highly praised by Christ himself: *"Amen, I say to you, in no one in Israel have I found such faith!"*[60]

The following constitute the principal responsibilities of our police and military men and women who, like the Centurion in the Gospel, profess their faith in Christ their overall commander:

i. They are not to take money from anyone by force or to accuse anyone falsely. They should be content with their pay[61]. This means that although bribery and corruption seems to be the normal way of life for most people who are serving in the military and police, the Christian will do everything to dissociate himself or herself from such scandalous practices, even if that will entail suffering, persecution or remaining in poverty or perhaps being the laughing-stock of others. It was to those who suffer such situations for His sake that the Lord said, "*Happy are you who are hungry now; you will be filled*"[62]. But as for those who extort money from others in order to satisfy their needs, as a good number of our brothers and sisters in uniform do in this country – even demanding bribes or gifts as a right granted them by their status or office – they ought to reflect carefully on our Lord's words: "*How terrible for you who are rich now, you have had*

[60] Matthew 8:10
[61] Cf. Luke 3: 14.
[62] Luke 6: 20-21.

your easy life! How terrible for you who are full now; you will go hungry"[63].

ii. The positions they occupy and the weapons they possess should not present a situation for them to be proud about or enable them to get their way by violence, for "*God resists the proud, but gives His grace to the humble*"[64], and His hatred is for those who love violence[65].

iii. They must take care never to yield to the temptation of obeying a superior authority in something that is contrary to the Law of God or the Christian values. Should any person or situation tempt them to do anything that is clearly against their conscience, it will be a virtuous and holy act for them to disobey, bearing in mind the words of Sacred Scripture that we must obey God in all circumstances not human beings.[66]

---

[63] Luke 6: 24-25.
[64] James 4: 6.
[65] Cf. Ps. 11 : 6
[66] Cf. Acts 5:29.

PART TWO

A MESSAGE TO THE PEOPLE OF CAMEROON

INTRODUCTION TO PART TWO

Your Excellency,

My Fellow Countrymen and women,

I wish to begin Part 2 of this book by sending you greetings of love. Peace be with you all!

That God loves Cameroon in a special way is quite evident. Not only has He blessed it with a great endowment of natural and human resources, but more than this, He, in His goodness, has blessed us with peace in spite of ourselves. However, it is worth noting that real peace is not the absence of war but the presence of freedom, justice and concern for the common good. This is a pre-requisite for any meaningful development.

As we prepare to throw ourselves on the immense task that lies ahead of us, namely, that of building a Cameroon of Greater Achievements as proposed by the President, I thought it would be helpful to write these few words which deal with some of the key concerns that burn in my heart. These have to do with the future and welfare of our country and people. I have no doubt that most, if not all Cameroonians, share these same concerns with me. So I consider myself privileged to write on their behalf. But above all, I believe what I have to write about concerns issues that are known to us all. I have highlighted a good number of them in Part One of this book. The President in particular, having been at the helm of this nation for more than three decades now, can easily see for himself that what I have to say in this book is what he is well acquainted with even if for some reasons, he has not yet been able to deal with them fully.

Your Excellency is assuming the office of President for another seven years term at a period in the history of our country and the world that I see as quite critical. All over the world, people's longing for freedom, economic and social prosperity, justice and peace have become much stronger today than in previous times. The 21st century citizen wants to be able to have a say in his or her own government and to participate effectively in the democratic processes that affect their day-to-day lives. Cameroonians, it must be admitted, are not left behind in this. They want to see their country growing towards real prosperity and development, not just in imitation of other civilized nations of the world but in order to be the pacesetter that it ought to be in Africa. By now it ought to be our joy not only to work for the betterment of our nation, but also to be able to provide needed support to the so many nations which are not as blessed as Cameroon. You yourself said it all when you expressed strong hopes that the country will become an emerging economy by 2035 and urged all Cameroonians to work indefatigably towards the realization of this great goal.

In line with the great aspirations you have for this country and which, as you are aware, are deeply rooted in the hearts of every Cameroonian, I have attempted in this little book to highlight, by way of a reminder and emphasis, those areas that your government will need to focus on in order to give real hope to Cameroonians. There is no doubt that our nation has a gargantuan potential and capacity for growth. In order to realize it, we all must work together as one people, each in his or her own way, according to how they have been gifted by God. But how do we go about this in the present circumstances, amid the numerous abysmal crises plaguing the country? This is what has prompted me to write this book entitled, *"Cameroon a Lion deeply asleep: Building a New*

Cameroon". It comes from the depth of the love I have for this country and the strong desire I have to see it become a happier home for its people and those who visit it. I hope that all will receive it wholeheartedly and see everything I have said in it against this background.

It is my humble hope that all of us who are privileged to be citizens of this beautiful and richly endowed country, Cameroon, will spare the time to go through this book so that together we will see in what way, in my view, we must collaborate in doing what is necessary to move this country forward. If certain things appear to be overstatements or understatements, I appeal that it is not so much the facts we must consider but the truth they are intended to convey.

May our God in His goodness bless us and all the people of the world.

FR. LINUS PATEM

Catholic University of Central Africa,

Department of Canon Law,

Yaoundé.

"The foundation of good government must be established on the sound basis of laws which protect the rights and define the obligations of the citizens. ... The Synod prayed fervently to the Lord that there would arise in Africa holy politicians — both men and women — and that there would be saintly Heads of State, who profoundly love their own people and wish to serve rather than be served." ***(ECCLESIA IN AFRICA, NO. 111)***

"... the Synod prayed fervently to the Lord that there would arise in Africa holy politicians — both men and women — and that there would be saintly Heads of State, who profoundly love their own people and wish to serve rather than be served." ***(ECCLESIA IN AFRICA, NO. 112)***

"The Synod also called on African governments to establish the appropriate policies needed to increase economic growth and investment in order to create new jobs.(218) This involves the commitment to pursue sound economic policies, adopting the right priorities for the exploitation and distribution of often scarce national resources in such a way as to provide for people's basic needs, and to ensure an honest and equitable sharing of benefits and burdens. In particular, governments have the binding duty to protect the common patrimony against all forms of waste and embezzlement by citizens lacking public spirit or by unscrupulous foreigners. It is also the duty of governments to undertake suitable initiatives to improve the conditions of international commerce. ***(ECCLESIA IN AFRICA, NO. 113)***

"Africa's economic problems are compounded by the dishonesty of corrupt government leaders who, in

connivance with domestic or foreign private interests, divert national resources for their own profit and transfer public funds to private accounts in foreign banks. This is plain theft, whatever the legal camouflage may be. I earnestly hope that international bodies and people of integrity in Africa and elsewhere will be able to investigate suitable legal ways of having these embezzled funds returned. In the granting of loans, it is important to make sure of the responsibility and forthrightness of the beneficiaries." ***(ECCLESIA IN AFRICA, NO. 113)***

CHAPTER 6

REHABILITATION OF OUR GOVERNMENT

6.1 Our Government Ministers

One of the key preoccupations of the President after taking the oath of office on November 3, 2011 was certainly to begin considering who to designate as Minister in his new government. These men and women are his closest collaborators. They are certainly the ones who, with the collaboration of the rest of the citizens, must work most ardently to enable Cameroon to achieve its goal of attaining real balanced development and prosperity.

As it is well known, some of these closest collaborators of the President, the Ministers, have failed our country woefully in the past. I believe the problem is that some of those who get appointed do not fully understand the meaning of the name 'Minister' which they bear.

As the name itself signifies, a *minister* is one who ministers to or serves others. Therefore he or she is a servant above all. But it seems that some of those who are privileged to be appointed do not understand that. As such they see their office as an opportunity to enrich themselves as quickly as possible before they are removed. As for the service they are appointed to render to Cameroonians they think little about it. They wish to be served rather than to serve. These are the sort of persons that should have no place whatsoever in our government. For, far from earnestly working with the President and other Cameroonians to achieve our mission of building the country, they frustrate it as past experience will have it. But since the mistake of putting a square peg in a round hole may sometimes occur even in this area, should there be reason to believe that any person who gets appointed into such an office in government is incompetent, corrupt or inefficient, it would be necessary that the President should remove him or her immediately. Meanwhile if there are any public funds that are unaccounted for or any damages caused by such persons, measures should be taken to necessitate the refund of all such money to the government treasury or cause them to repair whatever harm they might have been responsible for.

6.2 Appointed or Elected Government Officials

The Governors, Senior Divisional Officers, Divisional Officers, Mayors and Parliamentarians as well other government officials appointed or elected to serve in the various departments and branches of our government represent the President and the Cameroonian people in their respective responsibilities. It is therefore necessary that they perform their duties in consonance with the state's objectives and citizens' aspirations. This means that the people as such should be able to have frictionless access to them and feel free to call on them when need arises. On the other hand, these officials themselves should be in constant touch with the people they serve.

Many Cameroonians would recount, if they had the opportunity, the sad experiences they have had with some of these state officials. They make it so difficult for anyone to meet them and they themselves hardly go out to meet the people so as to see how better to serve them. People like these do not deserve to occupy any position in the government of our country. I need not mention the cases of those government officials who will offer no services that are not paid for directly by the citizens who approach them. Such persons will not put their stamp or signature on any document if some money they charge has not been given them in exchange. Unless they take a bribe they cannot render a single service to a citizen who is not their friend or family member. And yet, they are neither ashamed nor afraid to receive salaries from the state coffers at the end of the month.

I am not recounting here isolated cases which may be happening now and then or here and there. In fact, in order to be personally convinced of what is going on in a greater scale in our government departments and offices the President just needs to disguise himself and go to some of these places himself seeking to be served in one way or the other. You will be shocked at the reception you will get. In some places, if you hesitate to comply with their demands, be ready to be pushed out of the offices concerned. And so, the so called *Cameroonian way,* the very reason for the paralysis of our country, signifies that if you approach a civil servant's office desk or seek his or her service in one way or another, you do not come empty handed. If for example, they have to sign a paper for you to be awarded a contract or get any pecuniary benefits of any kind, be ready to assign them about 30% or more of the sum, otherwise expect nothing. And here we must ask the question: where is all this money going to? Certainly, it does not constitute part of the income of our government. It goes to appease the greed of a few at the detriment of the whole nation.

6.3 Transparency in Government

One of the key ways of eliminating inefficiency and corruption in public office will be to put in place and maintain an open door system, that is, transparency in the government of our nation. This is based on the idea that public office is not a private room but an open space where officials and citizens brainstorm and act on matters that affect the day-to-day running and growth of the nation. Things that are public ought, for the most part, to take place in public and not behind closed doors. I believe that if the President insists on such a system in our government, the transparency that this entails will help to curb some of the principal ills that are plaguing our government and country.

This entails, in my view, creating an atmosphere that is geared towards promoting and maintaining transparency and an open government. Government will, without doubt, usher in the revolution in mentality and social and economic development that Cameroon badly needs if the system is made an open one. Such an open system or transparency in government will guarantee increase in public participation and collaboration which are necessary in moving this country ahead. Transparency promotes accountability and provides information for citizens about what their Government is doing.

This will require that government takes appropriate action to disclose information rapidly in forms that the Cameroonian public can readily find and use. Government departments and agencies would also need to harness new technologies to make information about their operations and decisions readily available to the public. Such state institutions certainly include all Ministries, public and semi-public enterprises. In addition to the many well-known means of disseminating information, advantage needs also be taken of the great opportunity that the internet now offers the government for reaching the public. Besides providing up to date information on their operations online and through other forms of media, government departments and agencies should also solicit public feedback and learn how they could improve on their services.

In this connection, there is certainly the need for Cameroonians to get regular updates about the financial functioning of every government department and company.

This surely includes companies like SONARA and the Toll Gate services of the Finance Ministry. It remains a cause for much pain to Cameroonians that with the billions of CFA Francs that should be entering government coffers through the so many Toll Gates now spread all over the country, most of our roads do not reflect that of a nation which ought to be among the pacesetters in Africa in terms of economic and social development. What is even more worrying is the fear, easily verifiable, that most of what comes in as revenue from these places goes into private pockets. Since their functioning, like that of most of what is happening in the government agencies especially with regard to finances, does not enjoy enough transparency, unprincipled state employees are constantly sapping our nation of its vital economic power with impunity. As a remedy, there has to be regular and complete transparency checks and accountability with regard to income and expenditure in all government departments and agencies with Cameroonians having an eye and a say in all that goes on. This is to be accompanied, when necessary, with a timely intervention from the Executive and Judiciary in case of an abuse of public confidence. By so doing, inertia and corruption will be a far-fetched reality in this country.

6.4 Feedback Necessary

It is necessary that our President and our Ministers and all those who represent them should be as much as possible in constant contact with the citizens. If this does not happen, chances are that they may never get to know their minds; their likes and dislikes, their viewpoints, their suggestions, their concerns and problems. In the past it has been extremely difficult for the ordinary citizen to get in touch with them. Those who surround them form a type of cyst around them making it almost impossible for the ordinary Cameroonian to meet them. Most of these people cannot conceive the idea of an ordinary citizen coming so close to the President or

Minister, or at least getting their viewpoints across to them say by phone call or by approaching them in a ceremony or some other medium. Yet these are ordinary happenings in every democracy. This estrangement of the leaders from the led has served to create a gulf between them and the people they are leading. Having always to depend on others (intermediaries) in order to know what the people want from them cannot but do them a disservice since all these people, for greedy purposes, often make sure nothing comes to the knowledge of hierarchy except what they choose to let them know. This is to the detriment of the common good.

But, since in order for the President and his close collaborators to achieve the great task of leading this country to growth and prosperity, they need the effective participation and collaboration of all the citizens, it would be necessary that they put in place a system that ensures that they are constantly in close contact with the people. Most Cameroonians are concerned about the welfare of their country and they would quickly let the powers that be know when there are practices going on in government that can ruin the nation. If there are gross abuses of power or office or of state resources, this will be brought to their attention so that things can be redressed in good time.

The truth is that so many public officials have done their best in leading this nation into cesspit stagnation because they know so well that the President would never get to know about their corrupt deeds and negligence. For example, countless government contracts are not executed or executed very poorly and the money budgeted for them are embezzled and the projects are abandoned. Unprecedented levels of bribery and corruption avail in so many government offices and departments to the extent that they seem to have been the officially established norm of the government. Most of the perpetrators of these crimes against our nation are going on with blatant impunity because they well know that the Head of State will never get to know or find out about what is happening in their respective offices or stations. They can always find people to cover them up simply by sharing the booty with them even if these people were sent by the President himself to find out how things are going in order to report back to him.

There is now the common practice of misusing or selling state property or simply turning them into private use by so many of our public officials. There are countless similar corrupt and unpatriotic practices going on in government, and since the system that promotes this is a sort of network, whereby the junior official benefits because the senior one (the boss) is benefitting *albeit* illegally, there is hardly any possibility of the President getting to know what is going on unless the people who bear all the agony of such a corrupt system are able to get across to him directly. So His Excellency can see for himself how badly he needs this feedback from the citizens and the urgency with which he needs to put in place a system that makes this possible and ensures its practicality.

In order for his Great Achievement programme to succeed, the Head of State would need to spare no effort in visiting, in a manner and time of his choosing, every key project that government is undertaking. He himself can testify how often some of those he relied upon to supervise or run important works for the nation have failed him and the Cameroonian people. Therefore, if for no other reason, the need to stamp out laziness, negligence and corruption in this country especially with respect to state development projects, makes it necessary that the President undertakes such impromptu visits as frequently as possible. Since the fear of God and love for the nation unfortunately has vanished from the hearts of a good number of state officials or civil servants, it seems that this is the most important guarantee we have left and in fact concerning certain cases or situations it is the only one. Otherwise, not only will we be unable to realize our goal of building a Cameroon of Great Achievements, but, what is worse, we shall continue to witness our beloved fatherland being irredeemably crippled economically as its vast array of resources are gluttonously squandered by an oligarchy.

6.5 Getting Rid of the Spirit of Mediocrity

It's crucial that we to remind ourselves about one of the greatest plagues of our government and country; I term it mediocrity. Mediocrity is a well-known and vexing problem in this country. This is characterized by inexperience, indolence, incompetence, corruption and the sustained loss of skilled personnel. The poor quality of services provided by government departments, municipalities, other local authorities and of late the private sector, is a situation that has grown worse in recent years.

There has equally been a disturbing erosion of the service ethic even among professionals like doctors, nurses and teachers especially in the public service. Recent reports of children who were declared successful in the *Probatoire* Exam only to find themselves demoted some weeks later under the pretext of a computing error is just one example of the pervasive culture of incompetence and corruption in the public service that needs an urgent and more radical confrontation in this new era. In fact, the systems of education in use in this country, handed over by our colonial masters, have outlived most of their usefulness and clearly constitute part of the reason for the spirit of mediocrity that characterizes the lives of most of the citizens who are products of the system. We all can admit that our worst problem in this country is a mentality problem which shows itself in all aspects of the social strata. To solve that problem from its root, one of the key things that needs to be done is to radically change and re-orientate our system of education.

This crippling mediocrity in public governance and service delivery constitutes a direct threat particularly to our educational system and public health delivery system. Nowhere else is this better illustrated than in the failures recorded in the management of drinking water, sewage systems and electric power that have already cost lives. The obsolescence of most of our public and private infrastructure, their neglect and the lack of constant maintenance by those who live or work in them reflects the little love many Cameroonians have for this country. It is even reported that funds allotted for the construction or renovation of state facilities and infrastructure are hardly disbursed until those in-charge have been guaranteed a reasonable percentage for themselves. Similar negligence and corruption have led to the deterioration and even total breakdown of water treatment plants in many municipalities and as a result of this, in spite of the vast amounts of water sources in this country, many communities do go without good drinking water.

Scarcity of water brings misery to many homes, especially in poorer communities.

Even in the nation's capital of all places water has become such a very scarce commodity with whole parts of the city going without portable water for days and in some places for months. And what is occasionally made available by the national water company can only be consumed by those who desire to cut short their lives. One wakes up each day hoping to see some concrete measures taken by those in charge to arrest the problem, but often it seems there is just no one responsible. Negligence in grave matters of this kind makes it plain that our nation has now become a land of survival of the fittest. What an unfortunate thing to befall a people!

This spirit of mediocrity, however, has reached its peak with the practice whereby so many people, especially state officials are using the name of the party in power and of the president as a cover up for their crimes, neglect of duty, lethargy and incompetence. There is every reason to be wary about those who spend all their time singing out or writing motions of support to the president at every opportunity in order to curry favours like undue appointments. On the outside they appear to demonstrate love and support for him and his work, but how many of them truly mean what they say? Experience has shown that a good number of these people have skeletons in their cupboards or embark in this game because of the prospects of gaining some privilege or advantage which they fear they could not gain otherwise. To achieve their aim, such people can go to any length trying every means, which to them, is most suitable for flattering the President or their bosses in offices in order to win their favours. Account also needs to be taken of the waste of valuable time and resources in the whole process.

It is quite clear that such eye-servants are the sort of persons Cameroon of today does not need. They constitute a serious distraction to the President and a drawback to the growth of this nation. Our country today stands in dire need of patriotic, disciplined and hardworking citizens and if the

Head of State or any arm of government entrusts one with any office of responsibility his or her only joy and desire should be to focus on serving their fellow Cameroonians with the dedication and love necessary and not give in to all these dissipations. From the Bible, I find the words of admonition addressed by St. Paul to the Thessalonians quite instructive here:

> *'Whoever refuses to work is not allowed to eat.' We say this because we hear that there are some people among you who live lazy lives and who do nothing except meddle in other people's business. In the name of the Lord Jesus Christ we command these people and warn them to lead orderly lives and work to earn their own living.*[67]

---

[67]2Thessalonians 3:10-12.

CHAPTER 7

RIDDING OUR NATION OF CORRUPTION

7.1 The Ministries

The Ministries and the Ministers who head them constitute a life wire in the executive arm of government that is supposed to collaborate with the President to ensure the day to day running of this country. Since they are so many of them, the understanding is that work ought to be accomplished faster and more effectively, for as the saying goes many hands make work light. But the truth is that, whereas there are so many Cameroonians in our various ministries who are conscientiously rendering their country the services expected from them, there are so many others who see these offices as nothing but goldmines from where they can enrich themselves as quickly as possible before they retire or are removed. And sadly these are in the majority. You sense this immediately you get into any of the ministerial offices, from the national level in Yaoundé right down to the level of the sub-division.

The corruption that is taking place in our ministries is so terrible and multifaceted that to describe it would be necessary to write volumes of books. The simple truth is that the worst and most disturbing types of corruption in this country are taking place in these offices. In spite of all the efforts to curb it by punishing some key perpetrators, it is worsening. Some people have described it as an *infernal network*, first because of the wickedness that is exercised in the process and secondly as a result of the immensity of the number of those involved and the complexity of the manner used to extort money from poor citizens who solicit the services of their offices.

Honestly, for this country to forge ahead it will be necessary for the President, Senate and Parliament to completely overhaul the ministries, getting rid of individuals from every level who are the architects of this evil that is rendering our country handicapped. It is important to close up the so many offices and agencies that exist in name only and provide no real benefit to Cameroonians, and above all put in place a more trustworthy system that constantly reports to the President about inefficiency, corruption, wastage and redundancy.

7.2 The Taxation Department

The taxation department is one of the key places that needs immediate attention. Every citizen knows that the principal source of state revenue are taxes. If people and businesses do not pay their taxes or do not pay all of what they ought to pay, our government certainly will not get the money it needs to cater for the welfare of the citizens.

Presently, there are serious problems with our taxation system in this country that serves to promote corruption thereby making it impossible for all the money that should come through taxes to enter the state coffers. The first is that, the individual business agent is expected by law to declare to the state what taxes he is due. This means that if such a person makes a false assessment of his annual turnover and his or her taxes are calculated on that basis they are not paying the correct amount to the government treasury as taxes. And this is what usually happens with the bulk of those who bother to pay at all. There are a great number of mega companies and businesses in this country that pay little or nothing at all as taxes to government. Tax evasion is a major problem which needs to be handled as soon as possible, so also the worrying issue of under and over taxation.

There are so many who are under the delusion that because of their special relationship with some state officials or because of their attachment to the ruling party, they are naturally exempt from tax; they and their businesses. Their party cards are their tax receipts. There are abounding cases of people declaring huge containers of goods at custom posts as party materials, which are allowed to go through without paying a Franc to the state as custom duty. If the poor custom official insists on any payments, he receives threats of being reported to the Minister or some other state official as being opposed to the party or the Head of State. But on the contrary, everyone knows that these are the sorts of persons that are instead doing everything to give the President and this country a bad name and to cripple our economy. This is a typical example of the type of corruption that is having a terrible impact on our taxation system as a source of state revenue. That the businesses of certain Cameroonians suffer from over taxation or are altogether crippled because of their membership in opposition political parties is also well-known.

Let us however pass over to the worst problem which has affected our taxation system. This has to do with the tax officials themselves. Personally, I sometimes wonder if the President is aware of the situation as it is. The truth is that our taxation officials have wistfully put in place a practice in the taxation department that is similar to the sort that the tax collectors had in Jesus' time. If the amount due as tax for an individual's business is say 10.000 Francs CFA, they will charge 100.000 FCFA, if its 100.000 FCFA they will charge 10.000.000 FCFA if they are merciful, otherwise they would demand 100.000.000 FCFA or much more. Their trick, as is evident, is that when they charge a very high amount the poor businessman or woman, for fear of having their businesses being closed up completely, will plead with them for a rebate. Through this dubious means they are sure that when finally the rebate has been paid, they will be left with more than enough to fill their pockets.

That a bulk of what should enter the state coffers from taxes is swindled by so many voluptuous officials in our government is a common happening, which makes it a matter of urgency that in order for our economy to be revamped, as the President has planned, stringent measures have to be put in place to end this horrible form of corruption that has rendered the taxation system of our country unjust, ineffective and unaccountable. One key measure that needs to be taken is for government to immediately dismiss corrupt officials from office and ensure that they make full restitution of whatever they have robbed the nation of. As pointed out before, this restitution is of absolute necessity since it is strictly required by justice. Another could be for the property of the culprits to be confiscated and immediately sold out and the money recovered returned to the state treasury especially if it is established that such property was acquired with money that came through corruption. In cases of corruption or stealing of state funds, measures that do not include full restitution cannot do real justice to the common good.

7.3 The Customs Services

If the president were to find time and talk to some of our young people and ask them what profession they aspire to enter into in future after their education, he will be shocked at what he will hear. Many teachers can share this experience with him. A young boy or girl is asked in class about his or her future aspirations, and they declare with alacrity their passion to take the customs' *concour* and to become custom officers as soon as they leave school. And you ask why? And they tell you it's because this is the only profession in which they have the greatest opportunity to grow rich very fast.

Even many parents think the same way when they press their children to take the entrance exam into ENAM.

We may blame our youths for nursing such ambitions, but they have learned this just by observing what is going on in the customs department in our country. It is seen and acknowledged as the fast-track to riches. This also means that it has become, as it were, the heart of corruption in this country. And if the President wants to acquaint himself with the acuteness of the problem, it would suffice for him to visit two areas in particular: the Douala Seaport and the custom posts at our border towns. But it seems to me that he can live the whole experience by visiting the Douala Seaport alone.

The level of corruption that is going on at the Douala Seaport is of such a magnitude that if you were to witness it, you would think that the real coordinator of the customs services there is the devil himself and not people who are expected to serve their country and fellow citizens with love and concern. The grabbing, extortion and stealing taking place there is calamitous, for want of a better word. And what is worse, it all takes place so openly and daringly that it appears as something that is officially mandated by government. So much money (constituting about more than 80% of state revenue) comes into this country through this channel as a result of the huge economic activities taking place in it, but not up to half of this amount, enters into the state treasury; it instead goes into private pockets. If we add to this the immense amount of money collected everyday by these officials through extortion, confiscation and theft then you get a fair picture of the ruin these men and women are causing to the economy of our country. The whole scenario could, indeed, be described as a sort of official armed robbery.

7.4 The Police and Gendarmerie

In all honesty, the great services that are being rendered to our country by our Police and Gendarmerie forces, as earlier indicated, need to be acknowledged. And it was with joy that I learned of the special effort that the government is making to attend to their wellbeing so that they may be better able to do their job, which certainly includes crime prevention crime; pursuing and bringing to justice all those who break the law. They also keep public peace and order, protect the community and help to reassure the community that justice and peace are maintained.

But in spite of all these, our forces of law and order, as they are usually called, have lost a great deal of their reputation and remain in the public eye more or less as an embodiment of corruption, to the extent that all that is said above about our customs service could equally be applied to them in equal measure. The major source of this problem lies with the interminable love for money by a great number of these state officials. You will find them ready to do anything to extort money from the citizens including the use of violence and arms against the very people they are called upon to protect.

There is hardly any adult Cameroonian who does not have a sad experience to recount concerning some of these our men and women in uniform. Just to acquaint ourselves with a few of the countless sad experiences that I have witnessed personally. A poor woman lost her life in the Bakassi Creeks because, she was pushed from the boat into the waters by a Gendarmerie officer for delaying to pay her share of the bribe that they have made mandatory for all travelers using that waterway. She was unable to swim to safety and there was no one to rescue her from drowning. A university student was killed when the taxi he boarded was shot at in Muea by a Police Constable. A similar incident took place in Mile 4,

Limbe, where a young man was shot and killed for failing to meet the Police officer's demand for some bribe. Now these cases are not isolated. Even as I write these lines, there are countless police officials all over this country who are using all the means at their disposal, including arms, to extort money from vulnerable citizens.

One of the deadly weapons that has been in constant use by these men and women in uniform to accomplish their aims is an iron bar covered with spikes which they readily throw under the tires of cars that hesitate to stop and make the usual or customary *contribution.* Wherever you find a Police or Gendarmerie control post or checkpoint along our highways, know that this is the main activity taking place there. There are reports that at some of these checkpoints, especially at the very busy ones, not less than 5 million Francs CFA is collected as bribe each day.

Without doubt, in order for government to continue to nurture the peace that is so characteristic of Cameroon and its people and in order to succeed in setting this country on the path to real progress and development, the complete revamping of the Police and Gendarmerie services ought to be among the President's top priorities. This surely will include the following among others:

- The reordering and redefinition of what should constitute their function and how far they may go in its exercise.
- The institution of strict limits for the use of arms.
- The complete banning of the use, anywhere in our country, of iron spikes whether by Law Enforcement personnel or by civilians on the high way.
- The forbidding of the collection and giving of money to them on our roads.

- Other necessary measures that will ensure the application of anti-corruption laws already in place.
- Plant radars and cameras at all checkpoints and tollgates to monitor activities of commuters.

7.5 Our Schools and Universities

Our country needs to invest a lot more on education. Everything needs to be done to get the three ministries concerned with education as well as all the various stakeholders to work together to create a common set of academic standards that will define what it means for our students to be truly ready for college and the careers options thereafter. We need to put in place a solid teacher evaluation system that promotes and allows the truly competent ones to teach our children in our schools and universities.

We need to bring about a revolution in our academic system by placing a focus on teaching and learning. For this, we need to bring together the best minds we have in this country on education, researchers as well as all the approved providers of educational products and services and even dependable foreign partners in this field to join the great endeavour of not just reforming our educational system but to radically transform it. These men and women will be challenged to put their talent and ingenuity to work in order to equip students with the skills that the 21st century Cameroonian needs.

Presently, most of the students who leave the college or university in this country, if they lack the means to seek better opportunities in foreign countries, look forward to the next available public service competitive exam hoping to be employed by government. But we all know that it is neither possible nor necessary for the government to employ all the citizens. This is a fact that the Head of State and other state officials have often reiterated. But so far little has been done to stimulate other avenues. Therefore our schools and universities under the new system to be put in place should be able to equip our students with the knowledge and skills they need to fit themselves in the world of work as soon as they graduate without needing to look to government for employment.

In this connection, we must mobilize for excellence in mathematics and science education so that all students — not just a select few, or those fortunate enough to attend certain schools —should achieve much higher levels of mathematics and science education. Over the coming decades, today's young people will depend on the skills and knowledge developed from learning mathematics and science to analyze problems, imagine solutions, and bring productive new ideas into being. The nation's capacity to innovate for economic growth and the ability of our nation's economy to thrive in the global economy depends on a broad foundation of mathematics and science learning. Such solid and practical education is equally necessary for preserving a peaceful, prosperous and truly democratic nation.

But for this to be possible the President will need to put in place measures that would rid our schools and universities of all the corruption and mediocrity that have paralyzed our academic system and rendered it largely unproductive. A good number of the teachers in our public schools are not committed to their work. The practice of teachers awarding marks to students for money or sex in many of these schools and colleges is common. Many others skip classes for flimsy excuses or for no reason at all. It has now become common knowledge in most of our public schools that sometimes children are not promoted on the basis of merit but rather on some unfamiliar grounds. Many principals do not admit students into government institutions, of which they are heads unless they receive money from parents and guardians as bribe.

As for our technical colleges, a peculiar form of corruption exists there. Everyone knows that we cannot talk of technical education without technical equipment. Those colleges, especially the older ones that had had the necessary equipment in place for the training of young Cameroonians do not boast of having them anymore. Why? The teachers and school heads connived to steal and sell these valuable equipment for their personal profit. A classic example here is the famous Government Technical High School in Ombe in Fako Division, one of the oldest such institutions in the country. Over the years, almost all the necessary equipment and tools installed there for the training of our youths have disappeared. Today it is difficult to find in this country a properly equipped public technical school either because equipment have been stolen and sold by the authorities in charge or because the money budgeted for their purchase was swindled by some individuals in the ministry in Yaoundé or by others in the same network. These issues dampen the integrity of our teachers and destroy the educational system.

Effective education includes providing the best possible learning and teaching environment in all our schools

We can conclude without any fear and doubt that our schools, colleges and universities need overhauling. In addition to the reforms that are supposed to be brought about, measures will need to be taken not only to cleanse our academic institutions of all corrupt individuals and practices, but also to prevent them altogether in the future from ruining our school system.

7.6 Our Professional Schools

How can corruption be handled in our professional schools? It is a well-known fact that they are the principal breeding grounds for most if not all of the corruption in our government. In a good number of these schools, the established criterion for admission is bribery. You either have to secure a place in them through your connection with someone of influence in government or through paying the designated amount as bribe. There are cases of successful candidates who sat for the entrance exams and passed but were later replaced on the list of successful candidates by those who never sat for the exams at all, either because they paid higher sums or because they knew someone higher up. It is said that schools, like ENAM that guarantee candidates a more lucrative position in government upon graduation, demand a bigger envelope as *sine qua non* for admission. And here we are talking about huge sums of money in the neighbourhood of 5 million Francs CFA or more.

So it is evident that if one wants to kill corruption in government and in our country as a whole, one of key places where attend will need to be focused is our professional schools, for it seems as if this is where the whole cycle begins. When aspirants to the civil service bribe their way into these schools, they seem determined once employed by the state to continue this cycle of bribery and corruption, at least in order to be able to get back what they spent in getting in there and some profits on their investments. It is very normal to do so as the pidgin expression goes *"chop, I chop countri broke"*. Truly, if you were to closely observe the way some civil servants are attached to money at the expense of service to the nation, you will have no difficulty concluding that they are principally trained in these schools to be experts or professionals in corruption or looting , since that is what most of them appear to know and do best.

7.7 Our Hospitals

Another area so important to public welfare but which has been rendered ineffective through corruption is our health sector. Our hospitals do provide many opportunities for corruption, as anyone acquainted with the functioning of our public health system can testify. Money leaks from hospitals and the health ministry through false procurement of equipment and supplies, ghost employees, exaggerated construction costs and inflated hospital bills. The result is a depleted budget for other necessary health care services such as primary health care programmes.

Ultimately patients suffer, either because they are asked to pay bribes for treatment that is free, or because treatment decisions are based on financial motivation rather than medical needs. It is understood that public hospitals are principally for the poor who do not have means. But in Cameroon they are for the rich therefore those who lack the means have no access and are left to die.

I will like to illustrate this with a little but shocking experience I had recently in one of our Regional Hospitals. I think it deserves to be named: I mean the one in Limbe for the South West Region. An elderly woman had just had an accident that left her almost dead when we arrived at the scene and rushed her to this hospital. A few people who were with us helped place this woman on a stretcher but none of the nurses on duty that evening were willing to attend to her unless the sum of 15.000 FCFA was given to them. We begged in vain that they go on with First Aid while we tried to look for some money. It took the special intervention of God for this old mother, who was bleeding profusely, to stay alive the whole period that we went around trying to get this money. None of the nurses seemed at all interested in attending to her even though they all saw her bleeding. No doctor was called until this money came. Even after all this, the reluctance with which care was given to her was painful.

There are countless Cameroonians with worse experiences than this. Stories like this ordinarily do not come to light and yet they happen in our hospitals every day. Needless to say so many citizens have lost their lives because of such negligence. So one must wonder what our hospitals exist for.

The principal ills affecting our hospitals, like other services, are incompetence, negligence, inefficiency and corruption on the part of doctors, nurses and other staff. Concerning corruption in particular, the forms, it takes are as follows:

- Engaging in collusion, bribes and kickbacks in procurement processes, resulting in overpayment for goods and contracted services; non-enforcement of contractual standards for quality.
- Diverting budgets or user-fee revenue for personal advantage.
- Stealing medicines and medical supplies or equipment for personal use in private clinics or trade. The General Hospital in Yaoundé is a classical example, but the problem is common all over the country.
- Absenteeism of Personnel. Some do not show up for work or work fewer hours than required, while being paid as full time workers.

- Extorting or accepting under-the-table payments for services that are supposed to be provided free of charge; soliciting payments in exchange for special privileges or treatment.
- Abuse of hospital resources. Using hospital equipment, space, vehicles or budget for private business, friends or personal advantage.
- Favouritism in billing and spending. Waiving fees or falsifying insurance documents for particular people; using hospital budget to benefit select individuals.
- Extorting or accepting bribes to influence appointment decisions and decisions on licensing or certification of facilities.

Efforts to establish and promote transparency in our hospitals and health programmes in general can help reduce corruption. But certainly a lot more needs to be done here. Perhaps it may be necessary to set up a commission that would come up with proposals and recommendations on how we can redeem our hospitals and health ministry in general, eliminate corruption and put in place a truly effective and up-to-date health system that would benefit all Cameroonians, especially those with low income.

7.8 State Contracts

Corruption in the public contract sector in this country usually takes many forms. This includes bribery, deception (fraud) and misrepresentation of facts. This often happens during the contracting process. Generally, corrupt practices include the following:

i. **Issuance of fake contracts**: The decision does not follow a policy rational or an existing need but rather the desire to channel benefits to an individual or an organisation. For example, demand is created for a good no one buys or needs simply to benefit the owner of the company and his accomplices.

ii. **Characteristics** are made to favour a special supplier or contractor and not to properly address the need identified; ***Exceptions*** to an open bidding process are abused, leading to single source processes; ***Participation*** of relevant stakeholders is ***limited***, making it difficult to assess the need and relevance of the characteristics as they are defined.

iii. **Evaluation** criteria are not set from the start or are not objective, thereby making them prone to abuse. Where these are established, they are simply shoved aside when favourites come into play.

iv. **Contracting process: the *Invitation to tender*** (an open bid) is often either not publicized or not publicized enough, thereby restricting the number of bidders that participate; ***When short-lists*** are used, companies ***bribe*** to be included or to gain access to them; ***Invitation to tender is publicized*** but very little time is given to present offers, making it difficult for bidders without prior knowledge of the contract to present bids;

v. **Abuse of confidentiality** or lack of publicity creates an uneven playing ground for bidders; in single-source processes, lack of publicity or transparency leads to unjustifiable decisions; ***Bidders or contractors collude*** to influence prices or to share the market by artificially losing bids, or not presenting offers.

vi. **Contract award: *Evaluation criteria are not clearly stated*** in tender documents, leaving no grounds to justify decision taken; Evaluation ***bids is subjective*** or leaves room for manipulation and biased assessment.

vii. **Contract implementation and supervision**: ***contract changes and renegotiations*** after the award are of a nature that changes the substance of the contract itself; ***Supervising*** agencies/individuals are unduly influenced to alter the contents of their reports so that changes in quality, performance, equipment and characteristics should go unnoticed; ***Contractor's claims*** are false or inaccurate and are protected by those in charge of revising them; ***Subcontractors*** and partners are chosen in a non-transparent way that make them unaccountable or seen as channels for bribes.

The President will get a very big shock if he were to decide to go one day to inspect some state projects or contracts that have been reported to him as fully completed. The only proof that exists for the execution of many contracts in this country is money spent and papers colourfully signed; with little or no real work done. As you may already know, almost all the state contracts that are awarded by various government agencies in this country are wrapped up in horrible corruption and fraud scandals wistfully tailored towards benefiting the awarding agent and the contractor principally and not the country and the Cameroonian people for whose sake and on whose behalf they are conceived and given out in the first place.

It is established that once those in charge find that they stand to have no substantial personal benefits or kickbacks from a particular contract or that the contractor is unwilling to let them have a good percentage of the money allocated for the project, they simply do not award the contract at all or look for someone else who can meet their corrupt conditions. Similarly, the HIPC Funds have not had an impact in Cameroon because of this hidden agenda. The result is clear for all to see: so many projects that are undertaken are poorly done or abandoned and never carried out at all. The deplorable nature of work done on our roads in the name of repairs or construction is a glaring example among countless others. Almost all our major roads are deathtraps claiming numerous lives on regular basis. This crisis does not seem to disturb those in charge of the maintenance or construction of our roads.

Certainly, if public contracts or procurements are well-done, with transparency and efficiency as the watch word, the positive impact this will have on the country will be enormous. For instance:

- There will be value for money spent by government.
- The National economy will be stimulated.
- Strategic regional development gains will be achieved.
- Investments and investors will be attracted.
- Equity among disadvantaged groups will be promoted.
- The welfare of the citizens will be enhanced.

As a key way to deal with this problem of corruption in state contracts or procurements, which has become so acute, I would like to propose the strategy used by South Africa called the *Plan on Procurement,* which has worked so effectively for that country. It certainly can work well for us too if it is well implemented. The strategies in the plan on procurement are as follows:

- Well-defined regulations and procedures open to public scrutiny
- Clear, standardized tender documents
- Documents containing complete information
- Equal opportunity for all in the bidding Process
- Improved access to information
- Developed tender advice centers
- Broadened participation base for small contracts

- Unbundle large projects into smaller contracts
- Promote early payment cycles by government
- Develop preference system for Small and Medium-sized Enterprises (SMEs) owned by disadvantaged groups
- Simplify tender submission requirements
- Appoint procurement watchdogs or regulator
- Classify building and engineering contracts

And in addition to all these, it will be necessary to always insist on having substantial firsthand feedback from the citizens who are the beneficiaries of the contracts. Perhaps the newly created Ministry of State Contracts, as expected, will constitute another key remedy to this crisis. But that remains to be seen.

7.9 Our Courts of Law

Another area where the degree of corruption is disturbingly high and common place is our Courts of Law. In the courts, justice is bought and sold. Even after paying you are not sure of getting it if your opponent pays higher than you do. On the other hand, you simply may not get it when you need it. For instance, those who can pay their way can get away with murder while a poor tenant who is unable to pay his rents may be convicted and jailed. The daily routine in our country's courts is very pathetic. The courts are full to busting point with poor pitiful citizens while rich criminals stroll about to commit more atrocities. Most of our court Judges consider their offices, like is the case with a good number of our civil servants today, as business centres; no service is rendered without being paid for it. No true Cameroonian can reflect on the enormity of the problem without shedding tears. Most urgent attention needs to be given here too, for as it is said, no country can be admired if its judiciary system is sick. Indeed our judiciary in Cameroon needs a complete makeover.

We all know that our Judiciary and Legal officers as well as Barristers, notaries and bailiffs, as soon as they are absorbed in to the corps, and before performing their duties, take the following oath:

> "*I, (name of individual), swear before God and all men honestly to serve the people of the Republic of Cameroon in my capacity as a magistrate, to render justice impartially to all in accordance with the laws, regulations and customs of the Cameroonian people, without fear, favour or malice, and in all ways, in all places and at all times to bear myself as a worthy and faithful magistrate*".

If they were all going to abide by this oath, things would be fine for our law courts and for our country as a whole. For, it is certainly our courts that ought to be at the forefront of the fight against corruption and the abuse of human rights. But if they get so terribly overwhelmed by this malady themselves, where then are the citizens going to find hope and solace? It is clear that we need to speedily do everything possible that must be done to get our justice system back on its rails.

As part of the suggestions I feel privileged to offer on how we can combat and eliminate corruption in our Judiciary system, I have thought it necessary to include here the recommendations of the COMMONWEALTH JUDICIAL COLLOQUIUM ON COMBATTING CORRUPTION WITHIN THE JUDICIARY adopted by all countries of the commonwealth in Limassol, Cyprus on June 27, 2002. Copies of this document, I suppose, are available with those who serve in the judiciary arm of our government. If these are carefully implemented, they will certainly help bring about the sort of complete overhauling that our judiciary and the whole legal system desire in this country. Below are the excerpts which I consider of paramount importance to us.

i. Recommends the adoption of guidelines on judicial ethics as a means of underpinning the integrity of the judiciary and promoting better public awareness of the requisite ethical standards. Such guidelines should be formulated by judicial officers and kept under constant review by them. Judicial officers should take responsibility for ensuring compliance with those guidelines;

ii. Urges all national and international legal professional organisations within the Commonwealth to promote anti-corruption programmes for the legal profession;

iii. Encourages the formulation of national strategies aimed at eliminating conflicts of interest and corrupt practices within the judiciary;

iv. Recognising that transparency assists in combating corruption, encourages judicial officers and their court staff to foster greater public awareness of the court's operations, role and function;

v. Places on record its support in principle for the Latimer House Guidelines and their footnotes as they relate to the judiciary; and

vi. Notes that traditional or customary courts and other tribunals recognised in some national constitutions make a positive contribution to the administration of justice. The public that is served by such bodies should continue to expect and receive fair and just resolution of their disputes.

In considering action within the courts, the Colloquium expresses the view that:

i. Judicial training programmes should be available and should include training on ethical and corruption issues. For newly appointed judicial officers the practice of mentoring should be encouraged; and

ii. There should be greater interaction between judicial officers at all levels nationally, regionally and internationally in order to promote the best judicial practice.

The Colloquium recommends for consideration by law ministers and governments the following:

i. Recognising the interdependence of an efficient, impartial and accessible machinery of justice and the process of good governance and development, that governments should allocate sufficient resources to the courts to ensure their ability to provide that efficient, impartial and accessible service;

ii. The process of appointment and promotion of judges should respect the principle of separation of powers and reflect principles of transparency, competitiveness and merit;

iii. To promote the recruitment and retention of persons of the requisite integrity and competence, Governments should ensure at all times that the remuneration of judicial officers is fixed at a level that will ensure that they enjoy financial security during their tenure of office and that upon retirement they continue to enjoy such security.

iv. Governments, in the light of threats to the personal safety of judicial officers, should provide adequate personal protection for all judicial officers particularly those who are regularly required to adjudicate on serious criminal offences.

In order to strengthen judicial independence and integrity the Colloquium requests the Commonwealth Secretariat to facilitate the carrying out of a comprehensive survey of the methods of determining conditions of service of judicial officers throughout the Commonwealth so as to provide guidelines on prevailing best practices. The Colloquium notes the practice adopted in some jurisdictions of the determination of judicial salaries and terms and conditions by an independent commission.

In dealing with the issue of judicial accountability, the Colloquium:

i. Notes with approval that in some jurisdictions the judiciary publishes periodic reports of its activities. The Colloquium considers that this is a desirable practice for purposes of accountability and promoting greater understanding of its role.

ii. Expresses its view that there should be a greater degree of judicial awareness of the work of the court staff and liaison with the said staff should be encouraged in order to ensure the smooth operation of the judicial system.

iii. In order to maintain public confidence in the judicial system, recommends that the Courts should at all times ensure that their rules and procedures are simplified and that, except for a good cause, cases should be heard in public.

iv. Recommends that judicial officers should ensure that their judgments are well reasoned and delivered within a reasonable time; and

v. Notes that a pro-active leadership role of Heads of Judiciary is essential in promoting an impartial and independent, competent, efficient and effective judiciary.

7.10 Foreign Aid

Observers and many foreign aid donors have expressed worry that a good part of the money that our country receives this way contributes to the enhancement of corruption, as those through whose hands these funds pass misuse them for personal gain and as a means to ensure that they remain in their positions. It is estimated that about $35 billion in aid has been received in this country within the last 25 years or so[68]. This is money that could have radically transformed this country for the better if it was judiciously managed.

Personally, I do not think that the whole responsibility for this ought to be placed on the President's shoulders. The major problem, as I see it, lies with a good number of those that have been entrusted with positions of responsibility to serve our country in government, but who instead of sacrificing themselves for the common good are concerned about nothing but their personal and selfish gains. People like this have no qualms stealing money that could have helped develop our country and improve on the standards of living of all Cameroonians.

Now we find ourselves at a time when more and more foreign countries are either cutting or putting an end altogether to aid given to Cameroon. A glaring example is Great Britain which announced in March, 2011 that its aid programme to this country had ended. We cannot consider this as good news considering that Britain has been one of Cameroon's largest aid donors since independence. The present situation dictates that appropriate measures must be taken to ensure that whatever comes in as aid must be more strictly managed. It needs to be made known to Cameroonians and to aid donors that the reception and management of aid money, as with every other financial

---

[68] Cf. http://news.vanguardcameroon.com/2012/02/cameroon-economy-stagnated-by-bad_1469.html

transaction, is carried out with unquestionable transparency and accountability. And those who over the years have embezzled aid money should be made to pay back all what they have swindled. Some of them may be behind bars, but what is even more urgent is that all such persons be held to make full restitution of the aid money they had stolen or embezzled. There is no doubt that this is the desire of every Cameroonian who loves this country. This needs to be ranked as the first and most important strategy to follow in the fight against corruption, first because it is the key remedy required by justice, as earlier indicated, and secondly because that is the action that will immediately impact our economy and the lives of Cameroonians. And what is more, it will serve to build confidence in our foreign partners and investors.

CHAPTER 8

HONESTY AND ACCOUNTABILITY

8.1 The Present State of Affairs

Honesty and accountability are the two things that our country so badly needs. Every citizen ought to make these a part and parcel of his or her day-to-day life. These are the two things which, like corruption, embezzlement and inefficiency, have conspired to ruin this nation. And as a result, the name of Cameroon and its people have become an object of disdain and an emblem of shame abroad. These things have painted us all black, so that anyone who meets a Cameroonian for the first time by instinct becomes wary, because he or she is not too sure what sort of person they have before them.

One cannot introduce himself or herself as a Cameroonian anywhere in the world and expect to be trusted and respected. This is to the detriment of our country because in today's world, as we all know, there is hardly any individual, company or government that is willing to invest hard-earned money and resources in a nation where there is fear that it will enter into corrupt and dishonest hands. As the United Nations General Assembly observes in its document on Action Against Corruption:

> *"The seriousness of problems posed by corruption ... may endanger the stability and security of societies, undermine the values of democracy and*

morality and jeopardize social, economic and political development"[69].

Also because of widespread corruption and dishonesty that have become the order of the day in our country, people of other countries are not keen about visiting our country. On the other hand, Cameroonians generally do not receive a warm welcome in other countries due to this bad reputation. This, among other things, constitutes a serious setback to our tourism industry which is as a source of revenue for the country.

One Cameroonian mother recently told the story of the disgraceful treatment they received in Kenya while on transit. Their flight from Douala to Kampala via Nairobi suffered a five hour delay at that airport. So the passengers sought to take advantage of the long delay and move out to see the city of Nairobi. But to the shock and disappointment of this mother and the other Cameroonians on board that flight, permission was given to all the other passengers to go to town, but since they were identified by the airport officials as Cameroonians, they were ordered to stay back at the airport under the strict supervision of the security officials. Why did they receive such shameful treatment? It was because as the officials remarked, they know us just too well.

Corruption does show its ugly head in almost every aspect of life in this country and affects almost every one. Like a cankerworm, it has eaten so deep into the fabric of our society, paralyzing the economy of our country, social and political life, ruining our schools and universities and rendering our government itself ineffective. The lives of Cameroonians have been rendered weary and miserable as a consequence. The state of things is so bad that one senior citizen remarked that it appears that the only way to remedy

---

[69] United Nations convention against corruption: *Preamble*, (New York, 2004).

the situation and get Cameroon fully purged of this moral epidemic would be to physically eliminate every citizen from nine years and above. This may seem to be an exaggeration, but this remark serves to drive home the point that our country is very sick and needs urgent healing.

8.2 The Way Out

I am one of those Cameroonians who believes that in spite of the very bad state of things, there is hope for this country. But let us not pretend about it, this cannot happen without serious measures and hard work. As the saying goes, a critical illness requires critical remedies. As far as fighting and eradicating corruption in our country is concerned, I find the 1996 document of the United Nation General Assembly entitled; *"Action Against Corruption"* very necessary for immediate implementation. That document contains the *International Code of Ethics for Public Officials.*

It is worth noting that the document focuses on public officials, not because it is among this group of citizens that corruption begins and ends, but rather because if they are healed, the rest of the nation will be healed along with them. As the saying goes, "If the head is sound, the whole body will be in good health". If our country succeeds, as we pray and hope it should, to eliminate corruption from among our leaders in government and all public officials as well as from all public offices and government departments, there is no iota of doubt that the rest of the country will soon be purged of it with ease. Consequently, I have inserted in this book excerpts of the well-known United Nations document which provides the guidelines to be followed in the fight against corruption. If this is well observed in Cameroon, it will undoubtedly bring about the desired effect thereby providing the necessary impetus for our nation to rapidly advance towards development and prosperity. It is hoped that the President and all his collaborators, especially with the support of the judiciary, senate and parliament, can eradicate corruption in Cameroon and bring about overall efficiency in government. If every step is taken to ensure the effective implementation of the said *International Code of Ethics for Public Officials* which follows, this nation in no time will begin to experience positive transformation. For this, 'The fitness of every state official or civil servant to remain in office or for anyone to be given the opportunity to serve in our government should be determined by the extent to which they are able to faithfully abide by this Code of Conduct'.

International Code of Conduct for Public Officials

I. General principles

1. A public office, as defined by national law, is a position of trust, implying a duty to act in the public interest. Therefore, the ultimate loyalty of public officials shall be to the public interests of their country as expressed through the democratic institutions of government.

2. Public officials shall ensure that they perform their duties and functions efficiently, effectively and with integrity, in accordance with laws or administrative policies. They shall at all times seek to ensure that public resources for which they are responsible are administered in the most effective and efficient manner.

3. Public officials shall be attentive, fair and impartial in the performance of their functions and, in particular, in their relations with the public. They shall at no time afford any undue preferential treatment to any group or individual or improperly discriminate against any group or individual, or otherwise abuse the power and authority vested in them.

II. Conflict of interest and disqualification

4. Public officials shall not use their official authority for the improper advancement of their own or their family's personal or financial interest.

They shall not engage in any transaction, acquire any position or function or have any financial, commercial or other comparable interest that is incompatible with their office, functions and duties or the discharge thereof.

5. Public officials, to the extent required by their position, shall, in accordance with laws or administrative policies, declare business, commercial and financial interests or activities undertaken for financial gain that may raise a possible conflict of interest. In situations of possible or perceived conflict of interest between the duties and private interests of public officials, they shall comply with the measures established to reduce or eliminate such conflict of interest.

6. Public officials shall at no time improperly use public money, property, services or information that is acquired in the performance of, or as a result of, their official duties for activities not related to their official work.

7. Public officials shall comply with measures established by law or by administrative policies in order that after leaving their official positions they will not take improper advantage of their previous office.

III. Disclosure of assets

8. Public officials shall, in accord with their position and as permitted or required by law and administrative policies, comply with requirements to declare or to disclose personal assets and liabilities, as well as, if possible, those of their spouses and/or dependents.

IV. Acceptance of gifts or other favours

9. Public officials shall not solicit or receive directly or indirectly any gift or other favour that may influence the exercise of their functions, the performance of their duties or their judgment.

V. Confidential information

10. Matters of a confidential nature in the possession of public officials shall be kept confidential unless national legislation, the performance of duty or the needs of justice strictly require otherwise. Such restrictions shall also apply after separation from service.

VI. Political activity

11. The political or other activity of public officials outside the scope of their office shall, in accordance with laws and administrative policies, not be such as to impair public confidence in the impartial performance of their functions and duties.

Having considered this very important document, I would like to conclude this section with the following words of Jesus, who is the Hope of all nations. This teaching of His, clearly warns against the love and improper use of money which constitute the springboard for corruption and embezzlement.

> *And so I tell you: use filthy money to make friends for yourselves, so that when it fails, these people may welcome you into the eternal homes. Whoever can be trusted in little things can also be trusted in great ones; whoever is dishonest in slight matters will also be dishonest in greater ones. So if you have not been trustworthy in handling filthy money, who could entrust you with true wealth? And if you have not been trustworthy with things which are not*

really yours, who will give you the wealth which is your own? No servant can serve two masters. Either he does not like the one and is fond of the other, or he regards one highly and the other with contempt. You cannot give yourself both to God and to Money." The Pharisees, who loved money, heard all this and sneered at Jesus. He said to them, "You do your best to be considered righteous by people. But God knows the heart, and what rises high among humans is loathed by God[70].

Money is never to be treated as if it is our master; God is. Which is why He has threatened to exclude from His Kingdom all who love worldly riches more than Him, "*It is much harder for a rich person to enter the Kingdom of God than for a camel to go through the eye of a needle*"[71]and again, "*No one can be my disciple unless he gives up all his possessions*"[72]. If each public official and every citizen were to allow these teaching of Jesus to guide them in the acquisition and use of money, the terrible greed that has led to the widespread bribery and corruption in this country will give way to a wise use of all the resources which God has blessed our nation with thereby greatly enhancing the welfare of all.

[70]Luke 16:9-15.
[71]Matthew 19:24.
[72]Luke 14:33.

CHAPTER 9

THE ECONOMY

9.1 Government Revenue and Sources

Government has many objectives: reduce poverty, improve the living standards of our people and create jobs, provide the citizens with better healthcare, better education, and appropriate infrastructures. It needs to build hospitals, schools, and pay its workers e.g. doctors, nurses, and teachers. All these cost money. There are limits to how much Cameroon can raise from its resources, grants from foreign agencies or borrow from donors or the private sector in order to render services to its people. So raising revenues through taxes is necessary for government to have the money it needs to spend in order to provide more of these essential services thereby reducing poverty among our people.

9.2 Taxation

As earlier mentioned, our taxation department, is one of those departments that are suffering gravely from the corruption epidemic. Thus in its present state, it is risky to depend on it for the maximization of the tax revenue which our government so badly needs in order to carry out the laudable task of building the "Cameroon of Great Accomplishments." Depending on it would be like a family attempting to use a basket to fetch drinking water for the household. Naturally, one of the first tasks the government would have to embark on is to have the taxation system and the department in particular and the Ministry of Finance in general completely reformed. I think the president has made quite a good start in this direction by his appointment of the present Minister of Finance. From what I gather, this new Minister has already begun in earnest to put in place some key reforms. Nonetheless, reports of blatant and deep-seated corruption in that Ministry continue to fill the air every day.

The economic reforms needed in this country should focus on closing up all the holes that have been serving as leakages for money to disappear from state treasury. Whatever and whoever is judged not to be able to fit into the new system or endure its rigour should have no place in it. The guiding principle in the new finance management system for our country should be to make it impossible or a bitter experience for any individual or groups of individuals who would want to persist in robbing the nation of the vital resources it needs for its various development programmes.

Cameroonians all over the country expressed great joy at the President's recent declaration of a full-time war against corruption when he stated emphatically that "no one is above the law". I wish to say that when it comes to corruption, both the big and the small are harmful alike though to different degrees. In this regard, the President's searchlight would need to turn everywhere, including of course the Presidency itself, for we cannot surrender the welfare of so many millions of people to a greedy few.

It would be an achievement worth celebrating by succeeding generations to come if the maxim '*in Cameroon corruption is the normal way of life*' will fade from everyone's memory. This belief has negatively infected the minds of most citizens to the extent that in most places (schools, offices, homes, and even the church) the absence of corruption is considered an unusual thing. For example, if the President were to hear the terrible persecutions many civil servants have had to go through in their work places because of their refusal to take bribe or refusal to be corrupt, he would shudder. A good number of citizens have lost their jobs or been demoted from their positions or have had their files in the ministries filled with very bad reports due to their resolve to be content with their pay and to serve Cameroon in honesty and truth. These are some of the situations that buttress the need for you to put in place transparency in the new government. In this way, all such experiences will be freely brought to light by those who suffer them. And if there are ministers who knew about such things going on in their ministerial departments and they never dealt with them and kept the President informed, then they certainly do not deserve the privilege of ministering to the people of this country.

But coming back to the issue under consideration, it will be worthwhile to state that some of the key issues that need immediate consideration is the tax reform to be carried out so that the new system which is to be put in place should truly serve to mobilize and maximize revenue collection. This will give the government the economic power it needs to transform the nation and the lives of its people for good. In order to advance this course, here are my humble suggestions:

i. ***Avoid taxes that hamper economic development or job creation.*** Our new tax system should be designed to promote development and create jobs. If improving revenue injures development and impedes job creation, then it ruins the very foundation on which it ought to stand. The President would agree with me that this is exactly what the present system in place has done. A young university graduate, for instance, submits his papers for authorization to start a business. Even before he is ever able to receive any income from his small business, a tax of about 50% of his capital is imposed on him from the very start and he is threatened with closure if he delays payment. Just how can such a system help him stay in business or encourage other young people to enter into it? A tax policy like this, which has been existing in this country, favours unemployment and impoverishes Cameroonians. Bigger businesses should pay more while smaller ones should be favoured with smaller taxes and greater government protection so that they can be able to grow and expand.

ii. ***Policy on government revenue should concentrate on stamping out corruption and addressing the problem of tax evasion.*** Countless Cameroonians and businesses do not pay their taxes or do not pay what is just to the detriment of our economy. Our government is losing billions of Francs CFA every year through non-payment of taxes. Many factors account for this. The worst of them is bad politics.

There are many Cameroonians with mega businesses who simply do not pay taxes because they are ardent supporters of the party in power. This makes them unlawfully exempted from paying taxes. Their thinking is that since the government needs their political support, they cannot after all be taken to task over non-payment of taxes or any crime committed whatsoever. So many men and women in this country evade taxes and get away with it because of their affiliation to the ruling party.

There is a practice, which is so rampant now, whereby all kinds of crimes are covered up by simply going around in party uniform. It is well known that a good number of those who show excessive support for the ruling party do so not because of their love for this country but because of the various selfish advantages that their attachment to the party gives them. Of course, as earlier remarked many of those who go around singing the President's name and that of the ruling party which he heads are motivated by nothing other than their own greed. We can recall here the example I cited above concerning this business man who refused to pay customs duty on his containers of goods under the pretext that they were materials for campaign in his region. He threatened the custom officers that if they insisted on him paying, he would call and inform the minister, which one of them, he did not specify. Just because he used the name of the *party* and the *minister*, he was judged to have enough grounds for not paying his taxes to the government.

This is the common trend in this country today. The party has now become the hideout for so many corrupt persons who have no qualms robbing the nation of its much needed revenue. I believe the President's unequivocal warning against corruption and its perpetrators during the September 2011 party congress in Yaoundé and his firm resolve to fight it wherever it shows its ugly head in this country was a strong enough message to all such persons. But any tax policy that government can depend on to bring about a substantial increase in its revenue must be one that provides no room for official tax exemptions.

iii. ***A great deal of strain and complication is being created by our present tax policy because of the compulsory VAT***. I feel that while big businesses can pay it without much difficulty it suffocates smaller ones. Therefore it would be a big plus for the new taxation system and a great gain for our economy if smaller businesses are exempted from paying the Value Added Tax. There is even the impression that this tax renders the prices of basic commodities very expensive because of its being charged on each stage in the production chain. For instance, the buying price of a litre of petrol is so exorbitant partly because of this tax. Although the rich can pay the extra levies without missing it, it clearly has an adverse effect on the poor.

iv. Because ***harassments by corrupt tax officials*** are now so prevalent in this country, necessary measures need to be taken to protect taxpayers from their malicious actions. The over-zealousness they exhibit is not because they like their jobs but it is fueled by their corrupt intentions. Their actions are same everywhere. They levy huge taxes and charges on clients which cause the taxpayers to negotiate to give them a percentage of the total sum which is paid in cash to them. They avoid bank cheques because this can be traced and their corrupt tendencies found out. Many are reported to go home on a typical days with huge bags of money. Most have luxury cars, gorgeous buildings and huge investments at home and abroad not bought with money acquired through their own labours and sacrifices. They milk the state and citizens dry while their bank accounts continue to swell with this ill-gotten money. This can further be illustrated by the following experience:

Two people graduate from ENAM in the same year. One is a civil administrator and the other is a taxation or custom official. Shortly afterwards, the taxation officials grows into a multi-millionaire whereas the one in civil administration or the judiciary is still trying to build a hut to shield his offspring. This example tells the levels of corruption involved in this sector. Furthermore, stories also abound of the huge personal successes scored by those who work at toll gates in this country, which are still manually operated at a time when they can be electronically controlled to check fraud.

v. ***An electronically run system for taxation purposes can help a great deal.*** There is a lot of confusion in this sector as a result of non-availability of reliable data. For instance, it is difficult to state at the spur of the moment how many businesses and taxable persons and their respective categories are present in this country. This can be computerized and updated daily. This confusion is intentionally planted to defraud the government. It is important that government should sit up and use adapted and workable technologies to solve its immense problems. The way data is handled in this country leaves much to be desired. There is an attempt to hold back progress and the way files are processed in order to perpetuate fraud. There is no need to have decentralized systems of personnel management and still encourage personnel issues and other very crucial financial decisions to be made only in Yaoundé. This causes great losses at all levels. If government has to be credible, it must respect its engagements and be transparent in the way it runs its activities and personnel. Since the introduction of the e-governance programme not much has been achieved in Cameroon because many individuals who benefit directly from the present situation that reigns on the ground will lose out and government would benefit. The President needs to grind a few resistant heads and allow the e-governance project to take off full swing.

vi. Lastly, ***the government needs to ensure that Cameroon gets its own fair share from the exploitation of its natural resources by any national or foreign company.*** No exploitation that is not planned to substantially benefit this country economically, socially and environmentally should be accepted. Many have cried out loud that oil royalties should be paid to communities where these resources are extracted to ensure that there is equity in the way government functions but to no avail. There is no need for a company to be located in one council area and paying its taxes somewhere else. This breeds confusion and sustains a dangerous system whereby truth can be concealed and the real taxes due are not paid.

9.3 Salaries

There is a great need to increase the salaries and wages of the workers in the public and private sectors. The minimum wage of 28.500 FCFA is certainly not enough to sustain an individual for a month not to talk of a typical Cameroonian family. The inflation rate does not favour low income earners. Yet there are many employers who do not even bother to observe this limit set by law. So government needs to see what to do about these improvements and guarantee observances.

But what I wish to recommend here is that the President should endeavour to seek ways of raising the minimum wage for employees as well as putting in place a salary scheme that guarantees a better salary for all especially our teachers and health workers both in the private and public sectors. Similarly, it will be necessary to see about the fortification or implementation of laws that protect the rights of employees from being abused by unscrupulous employers. Often those who get so abused by such employers are the poorest of the poor. I am well aware that there are laws in place to ensure this, but like most of the good laws that we have in this country, they are hardly enforced or implemented by those who are their custodians.

For instance, the situation of the employees of the Tole Tea plantation in Buea Sub-division of the Southwest Region who for more than four months took up residence at the premises of the Regional Office of the Ministry of Labour and Social Insurance protesting the non-payment of years of salaries owed them by that corporation is a case in point. They were there day and night away from their families. They endured hunger, stress and the ravaging cold from Mount Cameroon. It was reported that no high ranking state official ever paid them a visit of solidarity. This sort of treatment speaks volumes, which need immediate redress.

The bad politics and ill-will behind all of these is so disturbing. It is actually something so mean that it does not deserve to be mentioned here. It is certainly not a blessing for our country that the poor should cry out for justice and their own fair share of the national cake and not get it because of the greed of a few. The words of Sacred Scriptures clearly point out that contempt for the poor and injustice towards employees and the marginalized quickly arouses God's anger and rob a nation of its blessings[73]. This is why we need to ensure that measures are put in place that make it impossible for the greed of any one person or group of persons to cause suffering or hardship on others, especially the poor and the underprivileged.

9.4 Privatization

The privatization programme that the government embarked on due to the severe economic crisis in Cameroon beginning from the second half of the 1980's, saw a good number of the big enterprises that were previously run by government handed over to private ownership. The key advantages favouring privatization as a means of redeeming the economy are clear to all:

1. Accurateness and commitment towards the quality of service.

2. Generation of more revenue compared to government enterprises, thus government can indirectly earn a bit more by leasing out enterprises to private organizations.

3. Customer support and satisfaction basically which is usually of much interest in private enterprises comparatively.

---

[73]Cf. Malachi 3:5.

4. Orientation towards profit and transparency in their functioning getting rid of hitches in conventional bureaucratic management.
5. Effectively minimizes corruption and optimizes output and functions.

But when one looks at some of the privatization deals that have taken place in this country, there is much reason to wonder aloud if the enterprises so privatized have registered these successes. Let's take the case of two of the more recent privatization initiatives: AES-Sonel and Tole Tea plantation, which were formerly owned by the government and the Cameroon Development Corporation (CDC) respectively. There was a great feeling of joy among the Cameroonian people when these companies were to be privatized and a well-founded hope that things would be far better with them than before. Much of that joy soon turned into a deep feeling of regret and sadness as there are lots of indications that things have gone even worse with these companies.

As far as AES-SONEL is concerned, many parts of this country have not yet been provided with electricity and those that have do experience sudden interruptions and power cuts now and then causing serious damage to property and putting people's lives at risk. Electricity bills have sky-rocketed and many consumers can attest that they are often hardly able to reconcile their monthly consumption with the sort of bills they receive, which is something that points to the deep-seated corruption that is still having a firm grip on AES-SONEL. Even the process of collecting payments for the monthly bills itself at their various offices is so disorganized and stressful that most people would readily want to terminate their contract with them had they any other alternative. What is difficult to understand is that this new company, AES-CORP, is an American enterprise and they know well that in the US the so many lapses that characterize their operations in Cameroon cannot be tolerated. They also know that the US has had uninterrupted power supply for almost two centuries now. They know for example that the frequent interruptions in the supply of electrical power that occur now and then in this country could never be accepted by American consumers who settle for nothing mediocre but always insist on top-standard services. I suppose these are the sort of services AES-CORP promised to provide Cameroonians during their takeover of the former government-run SONEL when it expressed its plans and determination to transform the electricity sector of Cameroon to meet international standards. Why then is it so slow to meet those standards after fifteen long years? Why can't they invest or transfer their technologies here? Why are they reaping from where they never sowed? Is it because the company has discovered that Cameroonians generally do not bother to insist on their rights and on quality of service?

As for Tole Tea, the situation is intolerably bad. Indeed, it is a classic example of a failed privatization attempt. It is so saddening to anyone who is acquainted with what is going on there. Presently, many cannot help asking why it was privatized in the first place and whether those who promoted this cause were not motivated by some selfish interest. This company under the new management has completely defeated the purpose of its privatization. Employees' living and working conditions have become worse than they were under CDC. As soon as the new proprietor took over, he had the houses of the employees demolished. Similarly, most of the employees were sacked but their accrued wages were not paid. This is a situation that has not been completely resolved since the takeover. For a company which because of the vastness of its plantations should have seen its employment rates go up has instead had most of its former skilled employees sacked. Presently, most of the tea plantation has been overtaken by wild grass. Currently, it looks like it has been almost abandoned to itself. Yet according to the management of the CDC, Tole Tea was the most lucrative of their plantations, and was a dependable and constant source of liquidity for the company. Tole Tea, represents not only a painful failure, but a glaring example of how the cankerworm of corruption has attacked the exercise of privatization in this country thus rendering it unfruitful for the most part.

My suggestion is that something should be done to rescue what can be salvaged. This may certainly not entail a government takeover since many of those companies that still enjoy government management like CAMTEL, in spite of their tremendous potential for growth, are not still performing as much as expected. Rather I think government should set up clear laws and guidelines that should be followed strictly by all enterprises providing needed services to the people of this country, both public and private. These Para-public institutions should be managed independently without political interferences. As for the Tea plantations formerly managed by CDC, one can hardly see any other solution apart from the fact that it should be given back to the CDC. Though it may be argued that such action would constitute a bridge of the contract signed, it is evident that by failing to run the company in the interest of Cameroonians they have themselves bridged a social contract. This is due to the gross exhibition of mismanagement of the company, which is so vital to our economy and the welfare of our citizens. The raison d'etre of privatizing a company, as we know, is not to consign it to the private benefit of an individual, but it is done so that it can be better managed for the common good. Once that focus is lost, the contract dies, as it indeed has in this case.

9.5 Agriculture

I felt quite moved by the President's new plans to give a special and unprecedented boost to the agricultural sector of our country, a programme he has termed *The Green Revolution.* It is particularly heartwarming to note that he is determined to kick-start the programme as soon as possible. But beautiful speeches cannot build a nation unless translated into action.

The use of modern means to increase our agricultural production is key. Once we are able to mechanize agriculture, the achievement of the great plans that government has outlined concerning this sector will come in no time: ensuring our food security and increasing our exports and reducing our imports in this domain. Cameroonians who have been privileged to travel to other parts of the world will surely agree with me that Cameroon stands out as one of the countries most blessed by God. There is hardly anything that any country in the world can boost of which we do not have in this country, even in abundance. Food resources, good climate and the fertility of our land are clear examples. In fact, Cameroon is the only country both in Africa and in the world in general where just any food crop does well. Bishop Immanuel Bushu of the Diocese of Buea is wont to make this remark that in Cameroon even if you throw seeds in the streets they germinate. This joke illustrates a deep truth about the sort of land God has blessed us with. It is not only the land that is excellent for food crop production but climate and weather conditions also favour food production.

I have often had the feeling that we have no reason to be poor in this country; there is equally no reason for some of our people to go hungry. What is more, there is no reason why so many countries in Africa and beyond, which are less blessed with these great gifts of nature, cannot depend on us to feed their own people.

I once was flying from Addis Ababa to Douala and had the opportunity to see from the air the terrible dryness and seeming barrenness of most of Ethiopia. This sight, which I did not quite enjoy, confirmed to me all the news reports I had heard when I was a child about drought and famine in that country. And the whole time in that flight, I kept asking myself why my country has not been sending food aid to the people of Ethiopia. Presently, we know that it is not only Ethiopia that is suffering from these undesirable conditions of drought and hunger. There are also others like Somalia and Sudan where we hear the death toll keeps increasing due to famine and hunger related diseases. It is because of plights like these which are plaguing humanity today that prompted Pope Benedict XVI in 2011, to make an earnest appeal for the intensification of food production worldwide.

In a message marking World Food Day 2011, broadcast over Vatican Radio, the Pope indicated that the tools which today's businesses and governments need to implement now in order to eradicate global hunger are investment in agriculture and, ultimately, the need to rediscover *"the feeling of compassion and humanity towards others, accompanied by the duty of solidarity and the realization of justice"*. He stressed the need for the beneficiaries of international cooperation to use any charitable contribution responsibly by:

> *"Investing in rural infrastructures, irrigation systems, transport, organization of markets, and in the development and dissemination of agricultural technology that can make the best use of the human, natural and socio-economic resources that are more readily available at the local level".*

And more recently, Pope Francis, in a special meeting with delegates to the 38th Biennial FAO Conference at the Vatican underscored the need to make food resources available to everyone. The Holy Father on that occasion insisted among other things that,

> *A way has to be found to enable everyone to benefit from the fruits of the earth, and not simply to close*

the gap between the affluent and those who must be satisfied with the crumbs falling from the table.[74]

My reasoning, therefore, is that in the domain of agriculture we have a very great challenge before us. First, we need to bear in mind that with agriculture alone we can radically transform Cameroon economically and socially. Thailand, for example, is fast growing into a developed nation depending principally on its tourism sector and rice production. I see it as a great example of how the efficient planning and management of a country's resources can yield enormous dividends. Obviously, with effective planning, mechanization, development and management of the agricultural sector, Cameroon can attain, within the next few years, a growth similar to that of many emergent nations like India, China, South Korea, Malaysia and Brazil. If it is better organized, the agricultural sector will give birth to four principal achievements:

i. Growth in employment even among the so many unemployed youths who will not resist the prospects of financial independence that the sector will offer.

ii. Immensely boost government revenue thereby bringing about the economic and social development so highly desired.

iii. Guarantee, or to use the President's words, "strengthened food security" for the Cameroonian people.

iv. Empower us to reach out with food aid to the so many hunger-stricken nations in Africa and even beyond.

Small and Medium Sized Businesses (SMEs)

One of the things the President and other top government officials have emphasized that is necessary to boost the

[74] POPE FRANCIS on FAO website: http://www.fao.org/news/story/en/item/178668/icode/

economy of Cameroon, as any economy at all, is the development of vibrant small and medium-sized enterprises. It is evident that there is no strategy more effective for creating immense employment opportunities than this. As Mohamed-Lamine Dhaoui of UNIDO (the United Nations Industrial Development Organization) asserts, *"the sector is key for employment, increased income, economic diversification, exports and foreign direct investment"*[75].

Presently, our country is not faring well when it comes to manufacturing which is so necessary for its development. The expansion of the SME sector will certainly entail the establishment of industries and factories engaged in various manufacturing activities. Whereas many African countries may have many difficulties in this domain, the potential for such development is very high for Cameroon because of two basic reasons: the great abundance of raw materials and the availability of a labour-hungry population. But as must be admitted, the development of the private sector in this country is bound to face some major challenges of which the President and most Cameroonians are well aware. The key ones are:

i. A difficult business environment, caused by widespread corruption, high taxes and long and complicated bureaucratic procedures in setting up businesses.

ii. Inadequate technical support services; that is, very limited technically skilled personnel. As the former Prime Minister Chief Ephraim Inoni once remarked, a

[75] ANDREW MUWONGE, *50 Years Later - What is the state of the African economy in post-colonial Africa?*, posted online on May 14, 2012:
http://www.southerntimesafrica.com/news_article.php?id=7079&title=50%20Years%20Later%20-%20What%20is%20the%20state%20of%20the%20African%20economy%20in%20post-colonial%20Africa

delegation of leading businessmen and women from South Korea, on an official mission to Cameroon, singled out the lack of the abundance of technically skilled middle class as the one key deterrence to foreign investment.

iii. Poor infrastructure and weak technological development. The sea, road and air transport systems which are so necessary in every industrial environment are poor, ill-equipped and inefficient.

iv. High costs for processing raw materials and non-availability of constant electricity supply. We are told regularly that SONARA exports its crude oil and refines imported crude oil in order to sustain its refinery. How is this possible? What is the logic in this?

These key challenges need urgent and effective attention if we really hope to make commendable and enduring progress in the realization of these great endeavours. It is the proper handling of these challenges that will give confidence to our local and foreign partners and investors.

Corruption in particular poses a very serious threat to the growth of our country. Corruption seems to be increasing in spite of all the efforts that have been made to combat and eradicate it. This presupposes that we need to change strategies used to combat it. CONAC has been doing a good job. But this epidemic has eaten so deep into the fabric of our society that to eliminate it much more is required. Despite all that has been said earlier on this problem; I think that for us to come out with a more effective technique against this ravaging ill, it would be necessary to let the people of Cameroon, through their elected representatives (the Members of Parliament and Senators), come together and deliberate on the problem. I am quite optimistic that through their brainstorming, recommendations and decisions, laws and strategies could emerge that would serve as more effective tool for the fight against this great enemy of our country.

Next, ways need to be sought to promote the development of technical skills in our people, especially the youth. I see no better ways of doing this than the revitalization of our technical education and professional school system. In this country, there is this misconception that only civil service jobs are worth one's years in school. Consequently, we see this tendency of young Cameroonians rushing to register for the next available public service competitive exam aimed at recruiting workers for the civil service irrespective of whether they are really interested in the office or function they are applying for or have the necessary aptitude for it. Most young Cameroonians in our schools have at the back of their minds this lone aspiration: to sit one day behind a desk in one of the government offices and look forward each month for a few thousands to enter their hands, which before the middle of the next month, they would have completely spent, with little or nothing left to save. Usually towards the end of the month there is this general slowdown that overtakes business activities in Cameroon. And when you ask to know why all you hear is *"les fonctionaires n'ont pas encore touché"*, that is *"Civil servants have not yet been paid"*.

The rush all over the country to submit documents following the President's announcement last January 2011 concerning the creation of 25.000 jobs in the Civil Service is proof that many view government as a bread basket for all instead of a basket each must labour to fill for the good of all. Many see government jobs as the be all and end all. Government has also made the conditions necessary for this thinking to thrive by allowing civil servants a lot of laissez-faire in the conduct of their affairs. The public sector has been made to be a place where people can do nothing and earn so much money. This is so true for those who have risen to the top where they can hold positions of authority and control budgets.

This outlook needs to change given the present exigencies of our country. I am of the opinion that government should not employ except if it is really necessary for the growth and wellbeing of the nation. This means that if government has to spend as much as 735 billion on salaries alone, as the new budget indicates, let it be for services that government cannot properly function without. It would be better for more and more opportunities of training in skilled and professional jobs to be given to young Cameroonians who constitute the greater part of the population of our country. Their empowerment is the principal guarantee for prosperity, considering the well-known Chinese saying that it is better to give somebody a line for catching fish instead of giving him fish. I presume that it is the implementation of this saying that accelerated the growth of China, Malaysia and South Korea which are all nations with which Cameroon enjoyed a strong trade relation but which also depended on Cameroon for economic aid some decades ago. Their sudden economic and social transformation has been the result of the effective technical and professional empowerment of the young and of the middle class. It is such professional training that will provide the labour force needed for the development and sustainability of our Small and Medium-sized enterprise sector, our manufacturing programmes and especially our research and development initiatives.

If we take the agricultural sector as an example, we see immediately the vast opportunities it offers for research, manufacturing and industrial development. There is reason for us all in this country to feel disturbed and even ashamed when we import high quality finished products skillfully manufactured from the timber, cocoa, rubber, cotton and bananas that we export to China and Europe. We have this wide variety of raw materials in great abundance. This is the more reason why we must have our people trained to transform them into products that will create a high demand in the world market thereby increasing our balance of payments surplus and improving the standard of living of all our people.

9.7 Government Spending and Contracts

I find government spending and state contracts some of the areas that need the President's attention and constant vigilance. These are the areas where one finds some of the worst forms of corruption and lack of patriotism exercised. It is common to hear some Cameroonians describing state funds as *meat without bone* and the manner in which many government officials play around with them says it all.

A government department, for example, organizes a seminar in one of the halls in Yaoundé or in Kribi and each participant goes away with a sitting allowance of 1million francs CFA. Now let's imagine that in one such seminar there are 200 participants, then 200 million will go away just like that in one day and from one department alone. If this seminar was to last for three days, then we are talking here of 600 million of state funds that I would say have been squandered. This sum does not of course include the amount used in the actual organization of the event which could even be more shocking. Note should be taken of the fact that we have not yet considered in this calculation, the huge and unknown amount that is budgeted but unaccounted for, which simply disappears into private pockets or people's bank accounts.

The scenario I have presented is just an attempt to sketch a rough picture of how public funds are recklessly spent in this country. Most of those who have access to government money in Cameroon spend it this way without any regard for the common good. More and more opportunities are sought for spending state money. And so in a typical government department in this country hardly is there any balance left over from the previous year's budget. Care is often taken that before the new year's budget is passed by parliament, what was programmed for the year ending has been completely exhausted whether or not what they were budgeted for have been accomplished. This sort of practice, so common in our government today, can safely be described as *official corruption.* This is therefore more devastating. Since the so many persons involved in it appear to be doing everything within the context of their day-to-day functions, they hardly believe they are doing anything wrong for which they deserve being taken to task.

Similar to this form of corruption is all that surrounds the conception and award of state contracts earlier mentioned. The general tendency is for those concerned or involved to have their own percentage of the money budgeted for the contract to be awarded. As a result of this, at the end the contract is either not executed at all or it gets done in a very poor way. No one, of course, questions the contractor for the poor or non-execution of the contract since those who have to confirm or reject the work have all taken their fair share of the booty. Even when the contract is carried out as stipulated another question must still be asked- at what cost was the contract executed and for how long? Usually, and shockingly, in many cases more than ten times the actual cost is spent on accomplishing a project or contract and for a much longer time than necessary.

Many state projects remain uncompleted like this for months and years

If it has to do with supply of materials or items, their cost is overtly inflated so as to allow everyone in the contract chain to have his or her chunk of the money budgeted. For example, you could find a packet of pens which sells at 2000 FCFA in a supermarket in town, supplied to a government office at say 90.000 FCFA. And if a mere packet of pens would costs that much, imagine what cost would be fixed to say a bag of cement. This is the sort of horrible corruption that characterizes almost all the state contracts in this country. Even aid money that is given by foreign government or agencies for projects that would better the lives of Cameroonians and foster the growth of our nation does not escape the greedy hands of this corrupt mafia. The mafia is quick to deny implementing any project that does not reflect their benefits.

I am sure the President is well aware of this most detestable practice going on in our government perpetrated for the most part by those who should be with him at the forefront of the battle against corruption. But if I highlight the issue here it is because it is a problem that concerns every Cameroonian and therefore all hands must be on deck to fight and eradicate it. And one of the key ways of doing this, and which I have already dealt with briefly, is by establishing transparency in government with regard to everything that is of public or common interest and which needs the effective participation and collaboration of the citizens for their proper management and realization.

CHAPTER 10

TRANSPORT

10.1 Our Roads

I have often wondered why our roads in this country cannot be like those we find in other countries even here in neighbouring West Africa where we have at least double-lane paved roads linking all major cities and well-constructed and regularly maintained network of roads leading to all parts of the nation. It is quite true that some effort has been made over the years in this connection, but it has been too slow and not far-reaching. Most of the roads in Cameroon are really bad even in major cities like Yaoundé, Douala, Bafoussam and Bamenda. There are dangerous potholes spread everywhere on most of our roads which, without doubt, contribute significantly to the regular ghastly car accidents that usually occur and claim countless lives.

Roads like this in many parts of our nation today make development impossible to attain

Roads like what we see in the picture above are all that many towns and villages in most parts of our country have to boost of. We still have many key towns and villages that have never known any good roads at all, making life extremely difficult for the inhabitants of these areas. It is thanks to some of these areas that Cameroonians are able to have food on their table. It is equally thanks to these areas that more agricultural produce are available for exportation to foreign markets for the benefit of our economy. The lack of good roads presuppose that farmers are either not able to transport most of their crops to local and international buyers or that they are compelled to do so at a very high cost. In the end, it is our country as a whole that is the loser.

There are many road construction or maintenance projects that were begun but stopped because both the contractors and those who awarded the contracts connived to swindle the money allocated for their accomplishment. Some were either not begun at all or done so poorly that within a few months of usage they were in a worse state than before.

Everyone knows that the Ministry of Public Works is officially responsible for ensuring that our roads remain in the best state possible. But being one of those government departments in which corruption has been so firmly established, it is not surprising why these roads are dilapidating at such a fast rate and no one seems to care. Even a very major highway like that of Yaoundé and Douala is in such a bad state that it has become a deathtrap for all using it. The recent maintenance work attempted on that particular road was so unskillfully and poorly done that it is generally seen as an open display of the incompetence, mediocrity and corruption plaguing public activity in this country. It is the same sort of scenario common with a good number of road maintenance works undertaken in many parts of Cameroon. But if the President were to announce a visit to some part of the country, everything would be done to give the roads and infrastructure there a good and befitting shape like it was done in Bamenda in 2010 and is now being done in Buea in preparation for the 50th anniversary celebration of the Reunification of Cameroon. Outside of such times, things are left in complete ruin. Just undertake to pay a surprise visit to most of our towns and cities beginning from Yaoundé and Your Excellency will see the roads largely covered by dust or mud, depending on whether it is in the dry and wet season. Water runways are similarly stuffed with all kinds of filth. Even in our major cities, you are going to find most of the roads impassable.

That good roads give birth to accelerated economic growth and a better standard of living for citizens cannot be overemphasized. Many times of late, the President has emphasized his intention to transform the roads in Cameroon into modern ones. It is hoped that, against this background care will be taken to ensure that paved roads reach all major towns of this country, an achievement that among other things will go a long way to prevent rural-urban migration. It is equally hoped that all our major highways will be widened so as to accommodate the ever increasing traffic. But in order that such noble programmes are not ruined or aborted as many have been in the past, it would be necessary to unravel the greed and corruption that have often characterized almost all major projects in this country and ensure that all such works are done and managed by those truly competent and trusted. Also this should be done in full transparency. In this regard, the method of awarding, implementing and receiving public contracts or projects needs to be completely reformed.

10.2 Road Transport Systems

i) The Poor State of Roads

As earlier observed, most of our road infrastructure is really poor and rotten. This has deadly consequences. The poor state of the roads is the main cause of road accidents in this country. If one has to look for the reason why our roads, even those linking our major cities like Yaoundé, Douala, Bamenda, Bafoussam and Garoua are so terribly bad, it is difficult to find any answer beyond the greed, corruption and the bad faith of the state officials concerned. Since most of them work with the sole intention of pleasing the President, as indeed some have shamelessly declared, once they are sure that their negligence and corruption cannot be discovered by him they feel free to do as they please. It is estimated that about 80% of the funds, both from internal and foreign sources, allocated for the construction and amelioration of our nation's roads go to the private pockets of corrupt government officials and contractors.

This caliber of roads do not befit our country much less our capital city

The very bad state of our highways, to say the least, give our country a bad image, deter foreign visitors and worse still breed many accidents on a daily basis. Cargo trucks and timber transporting trucks share the same narrow roads with small cars, motorbikes and pedestrians. This is clearly unsafe. Therefore, in their present state our roads do not present a good example of a good road transport system. Many of our government officials who run in the most sophisticated vehicles on these roads find it difficult to declare or admit, at least publicly that the roads are so bad partly because of the superb state of their cars which can ply all kinds of roads. If they were to decide to go around by taxi or use some of the buses plying our urban roads, their language would certainly not be the same. But let's hope that given the new policies being put in place, we will find ministers and other state officials thinking more of the common good than their private or personal comfort or interests.

ii) The Terrible State of vehicles on our Roads

Both citizens and foreigners to Cameroon have cried out aloud on the way public transport vehicles are overloaded with people and goods. The poor mechanical state of the vehicles themselves is also something that one cannot help mourning over. It is a regrettable fact which needs very urgent attention.

One still finds many vehicles of this nature on our roads transporting citizens and their goods.

Most of the vehicles imported into this country to ply our roads are near retirement and therefore are not road worthy, though they usually pass the so-called *visit technique* test due to corruption. A good number have been refurbished to look new without good engines and pedal breaks. These bad cars are imported into the country at high custom duties. This makes it impossible for vehicle owners to think of purchasing new ones since the newer a vehicle, the higher the custom duty in Cameroon. This ought to have been the reverse. There are cars using our roads that are older than 20, 30, 40 and 50 years. Of the many vehicles that get involved in accidents on our highways so frequently, how many are found to be new and road-worthy? Very few indeed! The ugly sight of old and broken down trucks and passenger buses at the corner of our roads, sometimes even occupying a quarter of the highway, is among the stresses that one is bound to endure when one travels on our highways in the country.

iii) Bad and Unqualified Drivers

The drivers on the roads in this country pose more trouble to other road users. It must be confessed that in most parts of this country, the citizens are stock with bad and unqualified drivers on our highways. With the common mentality that money can buy just anything in this country, there is the practice of selling and buying drivers' licenses. This corrupt practice brings to our roads drivers who are not drivers at all except for the fake papers that give the false impression that they are. In addition to this, the terrible disorder reigning in the road transport sector where individuals or groups of individuals take the liberty to create their own laws and enforce them with impunity is also very disturbing. Practices like this have become the order of the day. And what is more, during the peak periods of the year, urban and inter-urban transport companies and other vehicle owners gamble to make gains at the expense of the population. Drivers park and off-load on these narrow and dangerous roads as they will with impunity. The acuteness of the situation leaves no room for one to doubt the fact that the Ministry of Transport has lost control of the proper management of road transport in this country.

As has been said over and over, our roads in this country are a deathtrap and our road transport system is also as bad. There is every reason therefore to hope that within the context of the infrastructural, economic and social transformation of this country planned under the new government economic initiative code-named, a Cameroon of

Great Realizations, all the roads in this country will be given the form befitting a nation in the 21st Century and especially one which has celebrated 50 years of Independence. This also entails that a really good up-to-date road transport system will be developed. This will make it easy for Cameroonians to buy or import new cars, rid our roads of old and environmentally unfriendly vehicles and put in place efficient road safety measures that are bereft of corruption and are under constant surveillance.

10.3 Getting Rid of all Road Encumbrances

As part of the effort to restore order and safety on our roads, it is necessary that the many hindrances encountered on these roads should be carefully identified and removed all over the country. Chief among these are the so many police and gendarmerie checkpoints; both the permanent and makeshift ones that urgently need to be off-rooted to guarantee freedom of movement. It has been well testified that these checkpoints do not do this country any good. If anything, they serve to foster bribery and corruption. As if their presence and activities on the highways do not constitute enough problems to this country, they are usually known to mount old car tires, drums, sticks and stones on both sides of the road at these checkpoints. This way, they further narrow the small roads motorists have to cope with. These usually have disturbing consequences. These obstructions have been the cause of many road accidents which result in great losses of lives on our highways.

Road obstruction by Police and Gendarmes on our highways is now common phenomenon all over the country

Under the pretext of ensuring the procurement and possession of personal and car identification papers by road users, these officials have succeeded in setting up the worst corruption units in this country. It is well-known that at these checkpoints they collect money from almost every vehicle that comes their way. These places have also become in every way grave obstacles to safety on our highways. The numerous social, economic and physical dangers they pose to our country far outweighs whatever reasons could be found for keeping them at these checkpoints. Surely there is more than enough work for them in the towns and cities where criminal and security concerns are on the rise every day.

There is also the common practice of drivers with broken-down vehicles placing trails of uprooted grass on the road in an attempt to warn oncoming motorists of the presence of a dangerous obstacle on the road. If anything, this only adds to the danger and does not reduce the risk of accidents on our roads. These patches of grass that are often thrown on our highways, apart from the environmental hazards they constitute, often narrow the road and create deadly obstructions that have frequently resulted in several accidents and loss of lives. It is quite difficult to understand how the Ministry of Transport has been able to allow such deadly and abnormal practices. According to standard traffic regulations, there is an appropriate equipment, the red triangle, which is used in cases of breakdown or unusual stops on the road. This, of course, cannot be replaced by grass or tree branches.

10.4 Railways and Trains

The rail transport system is another area where a lot needs to be done in view of revamping it. The trains are very old, noisy, slow and bumpy. Citizens and tourists wishing to go round and do business or simply visit our country can hardly be attracted by them. Yet this is an area that could bring in a lot of revenue for this country if it were well organized. Getting new railways constructed and new and modern trains bought will certainly cost a lot of money but this will be money well spent. This will be recovered before long provided that measures to free this nation of corruption becomes effective and Camrail is freed of the corruption that has brought it to its knees, like many other companies in this country.

10.5 Seaports and Sea Vessels

Our seaports need to be developed to meet modern and international standards. The inauguration of the Kribi Deep Seaport project, which seems to have kicked off, is certainly a great step in this regard. But the lone existing Douala seaport is very much in need of a facelift. Draining the port cost so much. It is work that is subcontracted to a French company which has monopolistic powers over our resource base. This makes us dependent on them for our success as a nation which should not be the case. Kribi and Limbe provide less costly alternatives that can be used but something holds us back from exploring our potentials for the benefit of all. We need to hasten work on these ports o catch up on the lost advantages.

The Atlantic Ocean is an important gift of God to this country. It is a major gateway to Cameroon. It is certainly an immeasurable resource for development which so many nations that lack it could give anything to have it. The more we are able to develop and make proper use of it the better for the economic and social welfare of our country and its people. Therefore efforts need not be spared in developing the various seaports that we have, the principal ones being Douala, Kribi and Limbe. This will, without doubt, greatly ease the movement of goods and services within the Central African Region thereby enhancing not only Cameroon's economy but that of the whole region.

Cameroon also needs to acquire and run its own sea vessels. It's a sad reality that the few that were available and managed by the former Cameroon Shipping Lines were sold out. It is difficult to explain of what economic advantage it was to the country to carry out this liquidation. Everybody knows that a well-developed sea transport system, which certainly includes the ownership and proper management of commercial shipping vessels, is the pride of every nation.

10.6 Airports and Airplanes

Like the seaport, the air transport system is one key tool for economic development. This is something that is beyond the capacity of the government alone to handle. Private investors, both national and foreign, need to be motivated to get involved. Gone are those days when one could be brought to trial and jailed for attempting to own a private aircraft in this country. Most of the best airlines in the world are owned by private companies and not government. Let's seek to promote the same practice in Cameroon. We need to revitalize the air transport sector and revive the airports. We all wish to see Camair-Co grow from strength to strength. But we need to do much more in order to remodel and revamp our air transport. When one looks at other countries in Africa with ultramodern airports in all major cities and airlines with fleet of airplanes, one is bound to ask why Cameroon must be so terribly backward in everything.

Presently, the country can only boost of two major airports that enjoy international standard. These airports, are underused as only the few Camair-Co planes and a handful of foreign flights frequent them. But in order to really give the economy of our country the boost it deserves, create jobs for the so many unemployed Cameroonians and ease the movement of people and goods in and out of this country and within it, more airports will need to be developed and more aircrafts acquired through the joint action of state and private investors – both national and foreign. It will also be necessary to have airports constructed in all the regional headquarters and those that exist rehabilitated and put into full use. Easing the movement of the people around the country and out of it will provide room for cultural exchanges, economic, social and academic growth in a way that cannot be done otherwise. It's a scandal that it takes close to a full day to travel from Yaoundé to the North of Cameroon by train, which seems to be the only major means of transport to that part of the country that is available to the common citizen.

Everything should be done to eliminate state monopoly of the air transport system. For it is evident that when such monopoly combines with corruption as is the case with most of our state run enterprises, the outcome is usually devastating for the nation. This has been the reason for the collapse of so many companies among which we have the former Cameroon Airlines and Cameroon Shipping Lines.

The present state of the Douala International Airport reveals the depth of the ruin that corruption has done to the air transport system in this country. In no other country, not even in Africa, does one find so much dilapidation of infrastructure at an airport facility. In the Douala airport, necessary equipment are old and abandoned or completely lacking. There are no air-conditioning systems. Toilets are not available, and litter and rubble is visible everywhere. Over the years this is the ugly image that the once vibrant and beautiful Douala International Airport has assumed. Yet it is one of the major gateways to this country. Those in charge cannot be relied upon to care and improve things because the only thing greed and corruption enables one to do is to think of how to enrich oneself quickly at the expense of others. Clearly, one of the greatest tasks and achievements of the government will be to get rid of all these *wolves* from our public service system or at least to render them incapable of causing the harm they are often bent on doing to this country and its people.

CHAPTER 11

OUR YOUTHS

"The economic situation of poverty has a particularly negative impact on the young. They embark on adult life with very little enthusiasm for a present riddled with frustrations and they look with still less hope to a future which to them seems sad and sombre. That is why they tend to flee the neglected rural areas and gather in cities which in fact do not have much more to offer them. Many of them go to foreign countries where, as if in exile, they live a precarious existence as economic refugees. With the Synod Fathers I feel the duty to plead their cause: it is urgently necessary to find a solution for their impatience to take part in the life of the nation and of the Church.

But at the same time I also wish to appeal to the youth: Dear young people, the Synod asks you to take in hand the development of your countries, to love the culture of your people, and to work for its renewal with fidelity to your cultural heritage, through a sharpening of your scientific and technical expertise, and above all through the witness of your Christian faith." ***(ECCLESIA IN AFRICA NO. 115)***

11.1 The Situation of Our Youths

Cameroon is among those countries with the most gifted youth population in the world. Whoever takes the time to observe them as they engage in the various aspects of life will have no difficulty acknowledging the great capabilities with which they are imbued. But for our youths to reach their full potential and be able to make any substantial contribution to the shaping of their future and the growth of our country, there is a need for them to be given the necessary formation. The civil service approach to training is the worst thing that ever happened to this nation. All our children cannot serve in the civil service hence the so-called professional schools are inadequate and dangerously misleading. In Cameroon many are those who have stood still for years waiting to be admitted in one professional school or the other only to reach retirement age and be forced to fake birth dates to stay on course.

It cannot be denied that presently a good number of our youths are undergoing some form of training or another. There are so many, for example, attending school at various levels and yet a good number of others who are going through other forms of training in both private and state-owned institutions. But where are they heading to? Are they being given life skills training and entrepreneurial education to jumpstart the economy?

We need to admit that the sort or level of formation we are presently giving to our youths in this country is not adequate and does not meet the necessary minimum preparation they need. If, as statistics reveal, our youths constitute 60% of the general population of Cameroon and yet we find such a high level of unemployment among them, we ought to be really disturbed by the situation. The significance of this is that the formation they are receiving in this country, either in or out of formal school settings, is not adequate enough to prepare them for the world of work. Also, the fact that we find a countless number of them leaving this country to seek better opportunities in foreign lands means that there is a serious lapse with the sort of training that our country is offering them. Either the type of formation they need is altogether lacking or seriously inadequate.

Now, what is this *necessary formation*? In the opening Chapter of the Book of Genesis we find this command issued by God immediately after He created man:

Be fertile and multiply; fill the earth and subdue it. Have dominion over the fish of the sea, the birds of the air, and all the living things that crawl on the earth.[76]

This divine command does reveal the great potential that God Himself put in the human being when He created them. Man is naturally empowered to transform his or her life and the world in which he lives for good. But for this natural empowerment to bear the necessary fruits it needs man's own contribution which comes by way of formation or training. This training constitutes human empowerment without which the natural empowerment will not reach its full potential in the human person. So it is evident that the Western world is not more developed and advanced because its people are more gifted naturally than those in the underdeveloped world like Africa. To put it more clearly, the Whiteman is not more naturally gifted by God than the Blackman; certainly not. It is simply that governments of those developed countries give their citizens, from childhood, the opportunity to develop as far as they can, their natural endowments. This human empowerment naturally gives birth to human development without which no other form of development can be achieved.

Now, how far each person goes in this self-development process is not to be determined by society. The limit is to be set by the individual's own capabilities and this depends on how far he or she can go in taking advantage of the opportunities put at their disposal. Each person is called to take that path in life for which they feel gifted. The purpose of educational training is to enable them to attain adequate preparation for that. We are doing our youth and our country a grave harm when by trying to put everyone, as it were, in the same mold or compel everyone to seek the ready food on

[76] Genesis 1:28.

the table as if more menus could be made available simply by challenging individual thinking and ingenuity.

Communities need to provide healthy entertainment for youth and help them put their time into proper use.

11.2 Rural Urban Exodus

The problem of rural-urban migration is most certainly to be counted among the many that are plaguing the youth population of this country and having a negative social and economic impact on this country. When there is mass migration to the city, the migrants often find themselves faced with extreme poverty, poor housing, lack of jobs and little or no traditional family support. The migration problem also leads to a decrease in local farmed produce, thus increasing our country's dependence on imports. For example, I have often wondered why we import so much rice into this country when there is abundant availability of both land and human resource to enable us farm more than enough.

Concrete steps can be taken to address this problem which includes the following:

- For starters, economic incentives can be offered to the farmers to encourage them to stay on the land. Encourage the growth of food crops that can be sold within the country.
- More services, education, medical care can be offered in the rural areas.
- Provide credit facilities in rural areas to enable them have easy access to finance. That is, small loans with low interest rates could be offered to encourage the creation of more industries. For this, it would be necessary to revive and fortify those banks which have been set up to serve this need. They should be bereft of the terrible corruption that has paralyzed them and put under the management of competent and committed citizens. This alone can help keep rural communities at home, and create much needed jobs for people in the local or village areas. With the effective promotion of agriculture and farming, poverty will be eliminated among the people and their standard of living improved.
- Improve on transport and communication networks.
- Improve on infrastructural development by constructing modern schools and hospitals.
- Improve on security and provide security services in rural areas in order to promote peace.
- Make land reforms to enable the poor and low income earners get access to land.
- Educate people regarding the effects of rural urban migration and how they can develop themselves in the villages and empower them to do so.

11.3 Mass Exodus to Foreign Lands

It is a well-known fact that for a nation to grow towards the attainment of sustained development it badly needs the availability of both human and natural resources. The more important of the two, as was earlier emphasized, is the human resource. It is really difficult to understand how Cameroonians are able to endure the sight of the vast majority of our capable, talented and skilled citizens leaving their fatherland for foreign countries. Most of them will never return yet we keep entertaining dreams of attaining emergence.

Even as I am writing these lines, there are hundreds of young Cameroonians making their way either legally or illegally out of this country. We all know that this is the common trend. By what miracle do we really hope to extricate this nation from poverty and arrive at real prosperity without the brains and hands necessary to do this? So far, brain-drain remains one of our worst setbacks, but little or nothing is being done to redress it.

11.4 The Environment, Hygiene and Sanitation

As important as protecting our youth is the protection of the environment and the promotion of hygiene and sanitation. One big problem plaguing most countries in Africa and especially Cameroon and which, unfortunately, is not being given enough attention is hygiene and sanitation. It is often forgotten that healthy and morally upright citizens cannot be raised up in filthy environments. As one's surroundings is so does he or she think and behave. It is not for nothing that ancient civilization coined this dictum: *"cleanliness is next to godliness"*. This is very close to the Latin saying we have received from Christianity, *"anima sana in corpore sano,"* which translates to *"a healthy soul in a healthy body"*. Let us face it: where in our cities, for example, are we more likely to find an increasing crime wave and a high rate of juvenile delinquency? Is it in clean and organized homes and quarters or in those areas replete with slums and squalor? Of course in the latter!

Surely, we are concerned about forming youths of patriotic and decent character. For this very reason, we must have as a priority the protection of the environment where they live and grow up with their families. Due attention must be given to maintenance of proper hygiene and sanitation in all our cities and villages. What sort of discipline do we really expect to find in children who must spend all their days in dirty and stinking surroundings, living in homes with no clean toilet facilities, who are hardly able to bathe themselves and constantly go around clad in ruined and dirty clothes? Apart from the danger to health involved, who cannot see that decent behaviour is hard to instill in children and youths who live in such subhuman conditions!

I must confess that I often find it really difficult to understand our leaders in government who have had the opportunity to travel to foreign lands and seen the delicate care and attention given to hygiene and sanitation there and yet return with little or no zeal to try and do the same in their own country. Are we inclined to think that they do not consider their citizens worthy enough to enjoy those benefits which other governments consider their duty to provide to their people?

In order to preserve the sort of environment and discipline necessary to educate and bring up dependable youths who are the future of this country, the Government needs to attend to the following inter alia:

i. Set up schemes that will ensure the elimination of slums and filth in all our communities and help maintain the communities in a healthy and clean state;

ii. Provide clean public toilet systems at strategic places in all our towns and cities but also in the villages to prevent the pollution of the environment;

iii. Establish a programme that will ensure the education of citizens at all levels, in and out of school, on matters concerning personal and public hygiene and sanitation and the protection of the environment;

iv. Forbid the peddling of food items under poor hygienic conditions;

v. Forbid the peddling of goods and merchandise by children;

vi. Constantly see to it that all places where food and drinks are sold to the public are kept clean or closed down;

vii. Ensure that garbage cans are placed at strategic places and that all refuse are deposited in them and nowhere else;

viii. Conduct regular inspection of all public facilities to make sure they are constantly kept in good hygienic conditions;

ix. Forbid all activities that demean or damage the environment, like the indiscriminate felling of trees and burning of places, dumping of garbage in the waterways and gutters etc.;

x. Provide clean water in all communities. This includes re-establishing the public tap system and ensuring that individuals and families who want it can have potable water provided in their homes;

xi. Make basic amenities available to poor homes and children, especially rural areas;

xii. Institute appropriate sanctions against the abuse of the environment and the violation of public hygiene.

It is impossible to bring up responsible and disciplined youth in squalor

11.5 Empowering Our Youths to Stay back Home

Let's make sure that the mass exodus of Cameroonian youth or any citizen at all out of Cameroon should not be a cause of dishonor for the country but rather an honour. This dishonor can, and has usually, come about in two ways:

i. Seeking entry into another country illegally; that is without the necessary documentation or with fake ones;

ii. Travelling to another country when your country needs you more and when one could be better off at home than abroad.

It is both the responsibility of government and parents or guardians to ensure this. No Cameroonian should seek to be an embarrassment to his/her country and another by their attempt to escape into a foreign nation.

But what is more, everything needs to be done to encourage our citizens who are out of the country to return home unless they are clearly engaged in some service that is for the good of humanity and for the honour of our country.

Otherwise, there is no reason for them to stay permanently abroad. Let those who are idling abroad by all means return home and join hands in the common effort of nation building.

Many people, I know, will however take an issue with me on this since the reason for which most of our youths and other citizens are out of the country is not so much because they do not love to live in their own country but rather because conditions of living here have become economically hazardous for the most part. This situation notwithstanding, I think it would be better for most of our youths who are living out there, to return since their living condition in the foreign countries where they are presently lodged, is far worse than anything they could experience back in Cameroon. Secondly, I found a great deal of reason to hope for a better Cameroon for our youths when I listened to the President's inaugural speech of November 3, 2011, especially when I reflect on the words he addressed to our brothers and sisters who are in other countries. On that occasion he said:

> *To you of the Cameroonian Diaspora particularly, who are graduates of greatest institutions, plying your trade in world class firms, you who are excelling in the high-tech sectors, the time has come to put your skills at the service of your country.*[77]

When a leader of a nation speaks openly this way in a forum of this caliber he ought to be taken seriously. It is true though, that in the past other promises were made but were unfortunately not fulfilled. This could easily constitute enough reason for not taking similar ones seriously. But while I must admit that I am not capable of speaking the President's mind as to why some of the key promises he made to the Cameroon people in the past were never fulfilled, I wish to stress that the one thing that each citizen must never

---

[77] PAUL BIYA, *Inaugural Speech*, (Yaounde: November 3, 2011).

let go is hope and trust, not so much in ourselves but in God who gives us our citizenship in the first place. I strongly believe he loves our country greatly and will not fail to guide us out of the precarious conditions plaguing our beloved nation. He is the one truly guiding our country, like all others, albeit through the instrument of human leaders that take His place among us. Therefore, to lose hope completely of experiencing a change for the better in our country is to say that God is no longer in charge of the world which He created. This would clearly be blasphemy against Him.

Despite all these, we also need to always keep in mind this truth that God will not do for us what He has assigned or empowered us to do for ourselves. Though we have so much to complain about in this country, I urge that our attitude should not be like that of the paralyzed man at the Pool of Bethzatha. Jesus saw him at that Pool and knew well that he had been sick for thirty eight years – we have been sick since Independence – and He asked him if he wanted to get well again. Instead of simply answering yes and receiving the cure he desired, he began to multiply complains about his abandonment and misery[78]. I wish to say here that there are so many good citizens who are not contributing to the ruin of this country through corruption and other criminal practices but who are nevertheless helping to bring it down in two principal ways: despair and nonchalance. Dr. Kalam says, *"Evil thrives when good people do nothing".*[79]

Whereas despair is the loss of all hope that things will get better and that we shall experience happier times, nonchalance signifies the fruit of despair which is perception

---

[78] Cf. John 5:5-7.

[79] This slogan itself I believe was based on a quote by Edmund Burke, who was an 18th-century Scottish philosopher and a British parliamentarian. The original quote went something like, "All that is necessary for the triumph of evil is that good men do nothing".

of every effort to improve oneself or the state of affairs as futile. This therefore conditions the mind to remain unconcerned about whatever is going on, be it participation in elections, politics or activities to promote human and civil rights. But the problem does not end here. Generally, people who despair concerning temporal matters will almost invariably despair about eternal and spiritual matters also: their salvation, God's unfailing love and care for them, the existence of a better and everlasting world beyond this physical one and so on.

Now, both of these maladies contribute in no small measure to paralyze a nation and they both derive from lack of faith in God. That is why good citizenship requires a firm belief in God to strive and on the other hand one cannot claim to believe in God if he or she has no regard for their responsibilities as citizens. This is why patriotism is a virtue and the lack of it vice.

But what is this patriotism? Various persons have different views with regard to what it actually is. But the definition I find more to the point and closer to the Christian conception of patriotism is that of Teddy Roosevelt, the 26th President of the United States (1901–1909). According to him,

> *Patriotism means to stand by the country. It does not mean to stand by the President or any other public office save exactly to the degree in which he himself stands by the country*[80].

One who loves his or her country or a patriotic citizen tries to live by this teaching of Jesus: *"Give to Caesar what is Caesar's and to God what is God's.*[81]*"*What we are commanded to give to God and that which we have to give to Caesar come from one and the same provident God and both

---

[80] http://www.skeptic.ca/meaning_of_patriotism.htm
[81] Mark 12:17.

types of duty have Him for their source. Hence, our call is to accomplish both and not one in negligence of the other.

I have said all this in order to make plain the fact that we need not only complain about how wrong things have gone with our country without doing what we have the capacity to do in order to get things go better. God will certainly give us the mind and strength we need to think and do great things that will change our nation for the better but He will not and does not have to do the day-to-day toiling that such a change demands of its leaders and citizens. Thus, those of us at home and abroad should each see what can be done to move this country forward in every respect. It is true that the greed of a few have been a real obstacle to collective participation in the democratic process of nation building. And that is precisely one of the key reasons for which I have decided to write this letter in which I have attempted to indicate in what ways we can put corruption and those who persist in it at bay and move towards real progress. However, my mission, as I see it, has not so much been to indicate effective ways of solving our present crises and building a better Cameroon as that of causing a spark to be lighted in the hearts of all Cameroonians, so that from the deep reflections that this will provoke, great ideas will emerge on which we can build the future of this nation.

In line with the challenge that the President gave to our fellow Cameroonians living abroad, I wish to urge us to do what the Chinese did years ago with their own citizens and are still doing it today. Their government put in place a programme whereby funds and other necessary resources were made available to all citizens who had finished their studies or training but were still living in foreign countries for lack of better opportunities back at home. The scheme was designed to be so exceptionally attractive that there was hardly any skilled Chinese citizen that could turn down the government's invitation to return to China. We are witnesses of what economic prowess China possesses today in the world as a result of that scheme.

Dear all, I do not think there is anything that should impede our government from doing the same thing in order to encourage our skilled citizens abroad to return to their homeland and contribute in building it as you declared. Surely, you are aware that there are countless citizens abroad who have actually expressed their intention to return, but could not because of the grave and almost insurmountable corruption and bureaucratic red tapes that make it really difficult for well-trained and skilled citizens to achieve their dreams in this country.

Take, for example, the case of a young Cameroonian who returned from the United Kingdom with a Master's Degree in Electronic Engineering having specialized in Remote Sensing. He curiously went to the National Refinery Company, SONARA, in Limbe with an application hoping to be given the opportunity to keep busy while trying to establish a life for himself in the country. To his greatest shock, one of the officials in that company, whose qualification and skill, I am afraid, did not measure up in any way to that of the young man threw his certificate at his face while telling him off in a fury, *"On fait quoi avec ca?"* meaning *"Of what use is that?"* Being unable to withstand the shock and embarrassment, this young citizen who had returned to his country filled with joy and zeal and was eager to put his skills and education at the service of his nation, was forced to return to the UK where he is happily living and working right up till this day.

It does appear that there are many older citizens in government or other key services in this country who feel threatened by the very presence of young talents and brains around them. These fellows scare and would therefore leave no means untried to keep them at bay as much as possible.

But whoever such persons are, they need to be reminded that they cast a huge doubt on the quality and depth of their own education and training if the presence of other brighter minds, instead of providing needed opportunity for collaboration, fills them with envy and makes them quake with fear of losing their places. It shows that they are worthless in any case, I think that as we get ready to prepare the groundwork for our citizens in the diaspora to return and for young and skilled brains to actively take their place in the task of nation building, those demagogues and cynics who enjoy playing the game of drawing our country backwards should be prepared to be disappointed.

I have had the opportunity, since my childhood, of working with youths in various youth movements and for what I know them to be, if only government were to offer them the opportunity of gaining full self-empowerment through adequate educational formation, professional training and research and the means to put their skills and knowledge into effective use, each according to his or her own capacity, their collective contribution to the nation's development endeavour would be so effective and overwhelming that it will take less than ten years for Cameroon to become an emerging country. So let us count on the power and potential of our youth and the skills of our citizens abroad and that of every other Cameroonian at home in building, under God, a nation that squares with the dreams of its people. The President expressed this so aptly in the speech he delivered at the National Assembly during his recent inauguration:

> *As I take the oath, this day, before the Cameroonian people, I am convinced that TOGETHER, Cameroonians from all towns and all villages, at home and abroad, without any discrimination whatsoever, can, better still, must resolutely transform Cameroon into an emerging country, that is:*

- a country that creates wealth and distributes it equitably,

-a country that offers everyone equal opportunities for self-fulfillment,

- a country with strong and sustainable economic growth,

- a country with strengthened food security,

- in short, a country that ensures each and every one's wellbeing.

TOGETHER, we can, we must meet this challenge. I have committed myself to it. You have committed yourselves to it. The Cameroonian people have committed themselves to it. It is now time for action.[82]

---

[82]PAUL BIYA, *Inaugural Speech*, (Yaounde: November 3, 2011).

CHAPTER 12

LOOKING AHEAD

In line with this serious undertaking to which, at the President's behest, we have all committed ourselves[83], and in view of the collective participation that is required from each and every Cameroonian, be they at home or abroad, I wish to earnestly make the following proposal to the President and all Cameroonians:

- Call for a National Development Congress (NDC),wherein drawing an action plan Cameroonians of all walks of life will be carefully chosen to participate in The mission of the NDC will be to deliberate on the way forward for this country, taking into account all the aspects of development that both government and people must apply themselves to.
- Members of this congress will be Cameroonians drawn from all walks of life carefully. Our Bishops and other religious leaders in the country could be consulted to assist with the selection of members for this all important congress. The President may judge it expedient to also co-opt members from foreign countries who may bring with them the experiences of their country that can assist this congress in the realization of its task.
- Because the work of correcting the wrongs of our past and shaping a better future for this country is very arduous, I will have no problem if this Congress takes a whole month to complete its work.

---

[83] Cf. Ibid.

- The venue for this congress will be freely chosen by the President.

- Concerning the Agenda: this is the core of the matter. In order to establish an effective agenda that will guide the work of this congress, it will be necessary for the President to consult all the sectors that represent the views and interests of the Cameroonian people both at home and abroad. To this end, it would be necessary for him to set up a small preparatory committee whose task will be to work closely with the President in laying the necessary groundwork for this meeting. As part of the preparation, this committee will design an initial document that will be used to collect the views, suggestions and recommendations of the citizens. Among others, the committee will forward these forms or documents to the following groups or sectors: the Bishops and other heads of major religious bodies in the country; the various government ministers and other government departments or agencies; heads of major public and private corporate organizations; major NGOs, civil society groups, youth movements, women groups and trade unions; the heads of major banks in Cameroon; stakeholders in the educational sector in the country including student unions; and heads of all associations of Cameroonians living abroad as well as other groups or persons to be determined by the President. The list of those to be invited will be established in such a way that all Cameroonians are truly represented.

- All those who receive these documents will need to deliberate on them with their members and from their brainstorming provide information, within a stated time limit, to the organizing committee which will in turn synthesize all the information received and draft an agenda based on the minds of Cameroonians which they shall propose to the President for approval. The President may decide to study this draft agenda with a smaller group of people of his choice.

- If the president feels satisfied that the draft agenda truly meets the aspirations of Cameroonians and therefore constitute an appropriate working guide or tool for the NDC, he will then consider approving it, otherwise, before doing so, he may have to send the committee back to work again to polish up whatever he judges needs to be corrected.
- When the agenda is ready, the President can determine the date, time and venue for the NDC. At this point invitations preferably signed by the President will be sent to all the participants.
- The recommendations will constitute a necessary working document for the government and every citizen. It will map out the role to be played by each citizen in the process of building our nation and how and where they need to apply themselves in the life of our country.
- One of the major impacts this congress will have on our country is that it will serve to eliminate the art of pointing accusing fingers at one another and create needed rapport between government and people. Citizens will readily contribute whatever they can for the growth of the nation when they find that they have a clear say and responsibility in the running of their country and are constantly going to be updated on the work of government. They will and not only realize that they can make suggestions or recommendations to government that are readily taken but they can be called upon to carry out a function or task that will enhance the wellbeing of all.

- At the end of this congress, it will be necessary to appoint or elect a National Development Commission whose major task will be to work closely with the President and other government agencies and departments to ensure the effective implementation of the national development plans set up by the NDC. For that, it will need to meet regularly, possibly monthly or quarterly, to review every project or programme being undertaken in every aspect of development in the nation and then report to the appropriate quarters. This body will regularly update the President and the people of Cameroon on the progress of every development initiative in the country according to the guidelines established by the NDC. This body does not take away the work of government Ministers and other state officials, but it guarantees that there is effective rapport between government and people concerning the development programmes that government is undertaking. And what is more, unlike in the past, if there is an effective and adequate implementation of all projects and development initiatives living conditions of citizens will be improved and they will be happier. It will, without doubt, enable us to put an end to what the President painfully described as ***"poorly managed projects and failed commitments"*** which is at the bottom of the impoverishment that our country is experiencing.

- The guide to be established by the NDC will clearly highlight what our development priorities are in every domain and determine how and when they are to be accomplished.

- For now, I can hardly think of a better way for us to ensure the effective realization of the Major Accomplishments which the President has challenged us to realize. He keeps on inviting all Cameroonians to be more daring, more creative and more innovative. And if we work together as one people our collective efforts will not fail to yield better dividends.

GENERAL CONCLUSION

Having said all these, I have decided to add nothing more in this second part of the book *Building a New Cameroon*. What remains for me now to do is to bring this present write-up to a close. But before I do so I think it would be necessary to address a few words to those citizens and especially Christians, so many among us, who often claim that they have nothing to do with politics and consider all political, civic, social and economic matters affecting the country or society as something alien to them. Sometimes they even claim that *"politics is a dirty game"* and therefore incompatible with their Christian faith. Such people are wont to say things like: *"I am not a politician; I leave politics to politicians."* To them, I address the following words of the Sacred Congregation for the Doctrine of the Faith expressed in the concluding words of their document entitled; *"Doctrinal Note on some questions regarding the Participation of Catholics in Political Life"*, published in 2002 and addressed to all Catholics and people of good will all over the world:

> *The principles contained in the present Note are intended to shed light on one of the most important aspects of the unity of Christian life: coherence between faith and life, Gospel and culture, as recalled by the Second Vatican Council. The Council exhorted Christians 'to fulfill their duties faithfully in the spirit of the Gospel'. It is a mistake to think that, because we have here no lasting city, but seek the city which is to come, we are entitled to shirk our earthly responsibilities; this is to forget*

that by our faith we are bound all the more to fulfill these responsibilities according to the vocation of each ... May Christians...be proud of the opportunity to carry out their earthly activity in such a way as to integrate human, domestic, professional, scientific and technical enterprises with religious values, under whose supreme direction all things are ordered to the glory of God[84].

To the President and to all the good people of Cameroon, with whom I enjoy the privilege of being a citizen of this country, and their friends all over the world I, wish to express my deepest sentiments of love and respect, and pray our good God to bless each and every one of us and their families and keep Cameroon and all the nations of the world under the protection of His mercy. May the Most Blessed Virgin Mary, the Patroness of Cameroon, through the intercession of St. John Paul II, who loved this nation so tenderly, keep it and its people under Her maternal guidance and protection always[85].

---

[84] SACRED CONGREGATION FOR THE DOCTRINE OF THE FAITH, "Doctrinal Note on some questions regarding the Participation of Catholics in Political Life", (Rome, 2002), no. 49.

[85] We all know from the history of this country that on December 8, 1890, the Pallotine Fathers consecrated Cameroon to the Immaculate Heart of Mary at the first Mass ever celebrated on Cameroonian soil at Mariemberg, located in the now Diocese of Edea, designating her as the Patroness of Cameroon. They were the first missionaries to Cameroon, sent to implant the faith here by Pope Leo XIII. Also by visiting and blessing this country twice during his Pontificate, the only country to enjoy this privilege in all of Africa, St. John Paul II showed his special love for Cameroon. These are important facts we need never overlook or downplay as if they had nothing to do with the welfare of this country and its people.

EPILOGUE

This little work is primarily addressed to Christians as well as to all men and women of good will. But who is a Christian? It is necessary to point out right now before I delve into the main subject matter of the book that the noble name. “Christian” cannot possibly be home by those, who pay allegiance to occult or secret societies or other organisations condemned by Sacred Scriptures and by the Church.

One of these secret anti – Christian organization which are so prevalent in Cameroon is the Rosicrucian Order Society. And what is more frightening is that a good number of those who occupy leadership positions in the country are also members of this organization.

Undoubtedly, these secret societies like many others are also found in other countries in the world. But what is particularly disturbing about the Cameroonian situation is that it has almost been made official and membership into it is becoming mandatory, particularly for those in key government positions or offices.

“If you want to be guaranteed such a stable and lucrative position in government”, a prospective state worker or a new entrant into the civil service would be told, “you need to belong”. Belonging here means, the candidate should declare his or her intention to become a full member or swear allegiance to the secret cult. The worst thing is that this category of Cameroonians does not care about the general welfare of the common man. They care only about themselves. They are too greedy to a fault and make the wealth of the nation circulate only amongst their club members and friends. And of course, if a prospective employee values his or her Christian faith over and above temporary gains and pays full allegiance to Christ alone, instead of worshipping the devil, the Grand Master of all these societies, such a one is simply turned away.

A few other indicators of how these forbidden organizations are being made official in government to the detriment of our nation can be cited, but I prefer to pass them over. Most Cameroonians are acquainted, at least to some extent, I suppose, with the various crises that are plaguing our beloved nation. These constitute the reasons for its paralysis. But I think the worst of these crises is that of lack of faith. Whereas the Scripture says that success comes from God (CF. Psalm 88), more and more people in this country are being persuaded to believe that it is only by adhering to the Rosicrucian Order or similar societies that one can be guaranteed success. This false belief is made concrete and attractive, especially by the common practice of reserving certain gainful employment offers only to adherents of the Order, whereas those who reject it are simply ridiculed and denied such opportunities.

But let us face the fact squarely; a Christian who becomes an initiate or adherent of any secret cult renounces his or her faith in God and, therefore, bears the name of 'Christian' only in vain for the teachings and practices of these societies, particularly the Rosicrucian Order are opposed to the fundamental tenets of Christianity. This point needs to be made clear, especially for the interest of those who may be lured into these secret organizations without actually knowing what they really are.

Indeed, to show the grave evil that these secret societies, like all others, do and how irreconcilable their teachings are with the teaching of Christ, Pope Leo XIII of blessed memory, following his predecessors, warned that no one should think that he may for any reason whatsoever join them if they value their Catholic name, and their eternal salvation as they ought to value them. Among other things, he pointed out that in these secret organizations or groups is revived the contumacious spirit of Satan, together with this indefatigable perfidy and deceit. For this reason he instructed that Church leaders, together with the lay faithful should labour tirelessly to bring more and more into light their power for evil and to do all they can to correct the contagious effect of this fatal plague.

Consequently, Christians have from God, a serious mission and responsibility on their shoulders, which is as follows:

i) To Secret Cult Members:

Consider the need for you to withdraw from any sect or any secret society to which you may have given your allegiance, irrespective of whatever promises were made you or commitments that you might have made. For not, if you humble yourself and renounce the devil and his associations, and you offer yourself to Jesus with all your heart to take full possession of you and all yours. He will protect you and you will have hope of a truly successful and prosperous future.

What the devil promises and sometimes gives is all together counterfeit, which you will not only lose as soon as you have it, but which will ruin you completely, once you take possession of it. After taking this personal and heartfelt decision before God, look for the earliest opportunities to meet a Priest who will gladly assist you with your full comeback to God. When you become a true child of God after the image of Christ, seek to glorify Him and offer constant thanks to Him by using all the talents and gifts He has blessed you with to faithfully and humbly serve Him and your fellow citizens. The joy and desires of every true Cameroonian Christian should be to dedicatedly use all the means at his or her disposal to work for the growth of the

Church and the genuine development of our God – given nation.

ii) To Non – Members of Secret Cult

If by the grace of God you have not suffered the misfortune of being lured into a society of evil standing as many of our fellow brothers and sisters in the faith have been, do not make a boast of this. Had the Lord not protected you, you would have fallen into a lower and more miserable condition than them. As Christians, we are obliged not to condone evil. We are rather required by our faith to be compassionate towards those who are trapped by it. There is hope for every Rosicrucian member and all secret cult members who become fully converted to Christ, renouncing completely, their present allegiance and associations with the devil.

The key sign for determining if a particular organization is worth joining is to consider whether the Church approves of it or note. The Rosicrucian Order and Freemasonry are clearly condemned by the Catholic Church. There are many others that are equally condemned. Make the findings yourself to ascertain whether or not the society to which you may be a member is in good and favourable standing with the Church. If it is not, then all that is said above applies to you. You must, therefore, act as suggested. And all of us have a duty to pray for one another. Those who think they are stronger in faith have to pray even more for those who are weak. We should pray, especially for our country Cameroon that it may be a source of hope for its people and to those countries in Africa and beyond who are less privileged or not blessed by God as we are.

iii) To Young People

Make it a life policy never to yield to cheap promises. Our Lord says the road that leads to life (happiness) is rough and rocky and only few find it (cf. Mtt. 7: 13 – 14). Be determined to be among the few who find happiness through resting their hope in the one true God and hard work. No secret cult or society can give you the success and happiness that only God gives through Christ. So be persuaded that it is better to go hungry and jobless than to be full – belly and employed by giving away your rights, life and precious future to the devil and his followers. No one can ever be frustrated or miserable who has Christ as his only anchor. Yes, you may suffer for a time, but certainly not always.

And what is more, God is wont to train His own through suffering to make them better ready to embrace his Holy plan for them, so that when success and prosperity come, they will be better able to see more clearly that it was after all the work of God. Thus they will therefore, render him the thanks and worship that is due only to Him. He tried his only Son with suffering. Jesus could have yielded to the devil's promises if He wanted the easy way out in life. But He saw all the worldly glories put before him by the Evil One as too cheap, hopeless and empty, I believe we young people are each called to put Christ's example before us all the time, if we hope to save ourselves and our country and bring it to prosperity.

With these important points considered, let us now turn our attention to the main subject of this book which is "The Choice of our Leaders in Government: The Role of Christians".

BIBLIOGRAPHY

Documents of the Church and United Nations

AUSTIN FLANNERY, *Vatican Council II: Concilliar and Post Concilliar Document,* Vol. 1, (New York, 1986).

NECC, *Pastoral Letter on Corruption*, (Bamenda, 2000).

NECC *Pastoral Letter on the Economic Crisis*, no. 15, (Yaoundé: June 3, 1990).

NECC *Pastoral Letter on the Economic Crisis*, (Yaoundé: June 3, 1990).

NECC *Lettre Pastorale sur l'Engagement Des Laïcs dans la vie de la Nation,* (Ngoundéré: le 15 Janvier 1988).

NN., *Ex-Italian President Salfaro on the Lack of Christian Politicians* , in Zenith, (May 23, 2003).

PAUL BIYA, *Inaugural Speech*, (Yaounde: November 3, 2011).

POPE PAUL VI, Encyclical Letter *Populorum Progressio*, (Rome: March 26, 1967).

JOHN PAUL II, *Ecclesia in Africa*, (Yaoundé: 14 September, 1995).

JOHN PAUL II, *The Catechism of the Catholic Church,* (Nairobi, 1994).

POPE BENEDICT XVI, Post-Synodal Apostolic Exhortation *Africae Munus,* (19 November, 2011).

POPE FRANCIS, *38th Biennial FAO Conference*, (http://www.fao.org/news/story/en/item/178668/icode/)

JOSEPH RATZINGER, Sacred Congregation for the Doctrine of the Faith, *Doctrinal Note on some questions regarding the Participation of Catholics in Political Life,* (Rome, 2002).

UNITED NATIONS, Convention against Corruption: *Preamble*, (New York, 2004).

Articles and Websites

POPE JOHN PAUL I, In *Il Gazzettino*, (Venice: July, 1978).

ANDREW MUWONGE, *50 Years Later - What is the state of the African economy in post-colonial Africa?,* posted online on May 14, 2012: http://www.southerntimesafrica.com/news_article.php?id=7079&title=50%20Years%20Later%20-%20What%20is%20the%20state%20of%20the%20African%20economy%20in%20post-colonial%20Africa

http://news.vanguardcameroon.com/2012/02/cameroon-economy-stagnated-by-bad_1469.html

http://www.fao.org/news/story/en/item/178668/icode/

http://www.southerntimesafrica.com/news_article.php?

http://www.unescap.org/pdd/prs/ProjectActivities/Ongoing/gg/governance.asp

http://www.skeptic.ca/meaning_of_patriotism.htm

Le Cameroun

aux éditions L'Harmattan

Dernières parutions

DÉFAITISME (LE) DES JEUNES CAMEROUNAIS
Ngayou Tchoupe Gaël
Le défaitisme et l'inertie qui caractérisent depuis peu la jeunesse camerounaise sont les principaux défauts que l'auteur reproche à ses jeunes compatriotes. Mais eux qui ne trouvent plus de gêne à tout mettre sur la tête du gouvernement et à se définir comme les victimes sont aussi les principaux acteurs du changement qui fera de leur pays une nation comme ils en rêvent. Pour l'auteur, les jeunes doivent être auteurs d'une révolution qui leur permettra de prendre en main la gestion de la cité.
(Coll. Harmattan Cameroun, 27.00 euros, 268 p.)
ISBN : 978-2-343-04848-2, ISBN EBOOK : 978-2-336-36745-3

CAMEROUN, LES ORPHELINS DE LA RÉPUBLIQUE
ou la trahison des héritiers
Ngono Antoine Marie
Ce livre est une diatribe contre les élites dirigeantes du Cameroun, dont l'action égoïste a conduit, non pas à l'émergence d'un pays auquel la nature a tout donné, mais à celle d'une classe sans cesse croissante de laissés-pour-compte, les orphelins de la République, qu'il faut considérer comme une véritable bombe à retardement.
(Coll. Émergences africaines, 33.00 euros, 318 p.)
ISBN : 978-2-343-04468-2, ISBN EBOOK : 978-2-336-36803-0

GÉOPOLITIQUE (LA) DE L'EAU AU CAMEROUN
Ebogo Frank - Préface de Joseph Vincent Ntuda Ebode
La problématique actuelle des changements climatiques a précipité l'insertion et l'inscription de l'eau dans l'agenda politique national et international des États. En tant que deuxième province hydrologique et aquifère du continent africain, le Cameroun est au cœur des batailles de positionnement entre les différents acteurs intervenant dans son champ hydropolitique. Il est question dans ce livre de déconstruire les modèles figés qui ont été faits sur l'eau pour parvenir à une reconstruction des différents modes de gestion de l'eau.
(Coll. Émergences africaines, 46.00 euros, 466 p.)
ISBN : 978-2-343-04783-6, ISBN EBOOK : 978-2-336-36777-4

FESTIVALS DE DANSE TRADITIONNELLE AFRICAINE ET DÉVELOPPEMENT
Kamga Sofo Dominique
Préface de Pierre Fonkoua
L'Afrique est le continent par excellence des danses ancestrales. On remarque aujourd'hui dans le paysage culturel camerounais une effervescence et un déploiement extraordinaire des festivals de danse patrimoniale en son sein. N'y a-t-il pas, au-delà de cette mobilisation des foules, de sérieux mobiles qui sous-tendent l'agglutination humaine ainsi observée autour des festivals ? Si oui, de quelle nature sont-ils ? Peuvent-ils être d'ordre politique, économique ou tout simplement culturel ?
(Coll. Études africaines, 14.00 euros, 128 p.)
ISBN : 978-2-343-03843-8, ISBN EBOOK : 978-2-336-36605-0

COLLECTIVITÉS (LES) TERRITORIALES DÉCENTRALISÉES (CTD) AU CAMEROUN
Pour un développement de convergence rapide et efficace
Babagnak Gabin
Préface de Désiré Avom
Cet ouvrage indique l'ultime prix à payer pour un développement endogène, rapide, efficace et durable au Cameroun. Il s'attaque aux causes fondamentales de son sous-développement et apporte des solutions étayées par un ensemble de prédispositions et de valeurs éthiques et morales telles que le culte du travail, la méritocratie, la spécialisation, la division du travail, la mutualisation, la coopération, le partage des efforts, des risques et des bénéfices engendrés.
(Coll. Harmattan Cameroun, 14.50 euros, 138 p.)
ISBN : 978-2-343-04144-5, ISBN EBOOK : 978-2-336-36717-0

LEXIQUE DE 30 000 MOTS DUALA-FRANÇAIS
Ekotele ya 30 000 la biala ba duala frensi
Ebele Ekuala
Préface d'E. Ewombè Moundo
La langue duala est principalement parlée par les Sawa, qui constituent la communauté ethnique autochtone de la plaine côtière du Cameroun. D'après certains patriarches, tout Camerounais dont l'ancêtre patrilinéaire résidait sur le territoire allant de Campo à Mamfé, avant la signature du traité de 1884, peut se prévaloir Sawa. Ces communautés tribales revêtiraient aujourd'hui près de 6 millions d'âmes.
(Coll. Harmattan Cameroun, 25.00 euros, 236 p.)
ISBN : 978-2-343-03496-6, ISBN EBOOK : 978-2-336-36724-8

PROVERBES BÀSÀA DU CAMEROUN
Màngèn ma bàsàa ba Kamèrûn
Prix Kadima 2013 - Livre entièrement en bàsàa
Association pour les cultures vivantes et la précieuse nature - CUVIPREN
Préface de Henri Marcel Bot ba Njock
Les proverbes bàsàa présentés dans ce livre exaltent des valeurs, mais peuvent aussi servir à l'éclosion et à l'élaboration d'idées généreuses dans les domaines

les plus divers, en même temps qu'ils modèlent le comportement de l'individu. La langue maternelle, premier réceptacle de la culture, doit être l'objet de la plus grande attention de la part des populations africaines dont les identités culturelles sont insidieusement et gravement menacées.
(Coédition OIF, 12.00 euros, 96 p.)
ISBN : 978-2-343-05410-0, ISBN EBOOK : 978-2-336-36802-3

THEATRE PRODUCTION AND ARISTIC DIRECTING : LESSONS FROM BUBBLES THEATRE TROUPE
Tanyi-Tang Anne
«Tested on Bubbles Theatre Troupe in theatre practice and theory, this book vividly portrays Anne Tanyi-Tang's invaluable insight into the responsabilities of a theatre producer and artistic director. It will serve as a reference book on theatre production processes». Patrick Tata
(Coll. Harmattan Cameroun, 15.50 euros, 152 p.)
ISBN : 978-2-343-04315-9, ISBN EBOOK : 978-2-336-36496-4

CONTRÔLE (LE) DE GESTION DES SOCIÉTÉS D'ASSURANCE
Le cas de la CIMA
Fotso Jean-Marie
Préface de Roger Jean-Raoul Dossou-Yovo
À travers cet ouvrage, l'objectif de l'auteur est de participer au débat sur l'amélioration du management des entreprises, dans le cadre de la mondialisation des services en cours depuis la fin du XXe siècle. Il s'intéresse particulièrement aux entreprises d'assurance qui évoluent dans un secteur d'activité très réglementé, du fait de leur sensibilité sur les plans économique et social.
(Coll. Harmattan Cameroun, 39.00 euros, 396 p.)
ISBN : 978-2-343-04838-3, ISBN EBOOK : 978-2-336-36403-2

ESPACE (L') D'UNE VIE
Entre la naissance et la mort, les contingences de la trajectoire humaine
Ndjitoyap Ndam Elie Claude
Cet ouvrage aborde les fondements spirituels et temporels du vécu. L'auteur y énonce des idées provenant d'une quête inlassable des «profondeurs» de l'homme et aborde des questions essentielles qui ont vocation à régir les idées et le comportement social. Il fait «reliance» entre la vie et la mort par une appropriation pensée du temps, s'intéresse aux enjeux de la création et de la procréation ou encore à la problématique de l'euthanasie.
(Coll. Harmattan Cameroun, 16.00 euros, 156 p.)
ISBN : 978-2-343-04785-0, ISBN EBOOK : 978-2-336-36363-9

BAMILÉKÉ (LES) DE L'OUEST-CAMEROUN
Vaillance et dynamisme
Tiani François Kéou
Préface de Paul-Gérard Pougoue
Les Bamiléké sont un peuple qui vit à l'ouest du Cameroun, connus pour leur dynamisme. Ce livre présente un point de vue nouveau sur leur dynamisme, objet de nombreuses controverses ; pour cela, il s'efforce de le relire sous l'angle d'un

contexte d'insécurité, à partir de la «Préférence sociale pour la vaillance» (PSV). Il se veut être un instrument de développement durable de cette société, ainsi que de la promotion du tourisme culturel à l'ouest du Cameroun.
(Coll. Harmattan Cameroun, 18.00 euros, 172 p.)
ISBN : 978-2-343-04563-4, ISBN EBOOK : 978-2-336-36139-0

SUCRERIES DE CANNE EN AFRIQUE SUBSAHARIENNE
Procédés et métiers
Kapseu César, Ahmed Ali, Mingo Ghogomu Paul, Mbofung Carl, Ndong Essengue Guy Martial
Préface de Louis Yinda ; Postface de Paul Heni Amvam Zollo
Cet ouvrage dresse un état complet des connaissances sur la sucrerie de canne et ses métiers, un processus qui permet de produire du sucre à partir de la canne mais également de produire de l'énergie sous forme de cogénération à partir de la bagasse. Il traite de tous les aspects fondamentaux des opérations unitaires, technologiques et des métiers. Une large place y est consacrée au génie des procédés.
(Coll. Harmattan Cameroun, 27.00 euros, 264 p.)
ISBN : 978-2-343-04564-1, ISBN EBOOK : 978-2-336-36080-5

MÉDECINE (LA) CHEZ LES PEULS DU CAMEROUN SEPTENTRIONAL (1754-2013)
Mengue Me Ndongo Jean Paulin
Préface de Hamadou Adama
Voici mis au jour plusieurs aspects de la société peule d'hier et d'aujourd'hui. Cette société jouissant d'un grand équilibre ne peut être réduite aux activités pastorales. Elle regorge de connaissances endogènes autant dans ce domaine que dans ceux de la pharmacopée et de la médecine traditionnelle ou historique.
(Coll. Harmattan Cameroun, 47.00 euros, 480 p.)
ISBN : 978-2-343-02680-0, ISBN EBOOK : 978-2-336-35735-5

ESSAIS (LES) DE MONGO BETI : DÉVELOPPEMENT ET INDÉPENDANCE VÉRITABLE DE L'AFRIQUE NOIRE FRANCOPHONE
Esquisse d'analyse de contenu
Owono-Kouma Auguste
Préface de Lucien Ayissi
Cette étude s'intéresse à la principale condition du développement en Afrique noire francophone selon Mongo Beti : bouter la France dehors, mais aussi à ses propositions en vue de la sortie du sous-continent francophone de l'impasse dans laquelle l'a installé l'ancienne puissance coloniale. Le rapport de la tutelle française au sous-développement durable en Afrique noire francophone est, en effet, l'un des thèmes dominants des essais de Mongo Beti.
(Coll. Harmattan Cameroun, 22.00 euros, 212 p.)
ISBN : 978-2-343-03876-6, ISBN EBOOK : 978-2-336-35779-9

L'HARMATTAN ITALIA
Via Degli Artisti 15; 10124 Torino

L'HARMATTAN HONGRIE
Könyvesbolt ; Kossuth L. u. 14-16
1053 Budapest

L'HARMATTAN KINSHASA
185, avenue Nyangwe
Commune de Lingwala
Kinshasa, R.D. Congo
(00243) 998697603 ou (00243) 999229662

L'HARMATTAN CONGO
67, av. E. P. Lumumba
Bât. – Congo Pharmacie (Bib. Nat.)
BP2874 Brazzaville
harmattan.congo@yahoo.fr

L'HARMATTAN GUINÉE
Almamya Rue KA 028, en face
du restaurant Le Cèdre
OKB agency BP 3470 Conakry
(00224) 657 20 85 08 / 664 28 91 96
harmattanguinee@yahoo.fr

L'HARMATTAN MALI
Rue 73, Porte 536, Niamakoro,
Cité Unicef, Bamako
Tél. 00 (223) 20205724 / +(223) 76378082
poudiougopaul@yahoo.fr
pp.harmattan@gmail.com

L'HARMATTAN CAMEROUN
BP 11486
Face à la SNI, immeuble Don Bosco
Yaoundé
(00237) 99 76 61 66
harmattancam@yahoo.fr

L'HARMATTAN CÔTE D'IVOIRE
Résidence Karl / cité des arts
Abidjan-Cocody 03 BP 1588 Abidjan 03
(00225) 05 77 87 31
etien_nda@yahoo.fr

L'HARMATTAN BURKINA
Penou Achille Some
Ouagadougou
(+226) 70 26 88 27

L'HARMATTAN SÉNÉGAL
10 VDN en face Mermoz, après le pont de Fann
BP 45034 Dakar Fann
33 825 98 58 / 33 860 9858
senharmattan@gmail.com / senlibraire@gmail.com
www.harmattansenegal.com

L'HARMATTAN BÉNIN
ISOR-BENIN
01 BP 359 COTONOU-RP
Quartier Gbèdjromèdé,
Rue Agbélenco, Lot 1247 I
Tél : 00 229 21 32 53 79
christian_dablaka123@yahoo.fr

Achevé d'imprimer par Corlet Numérique - 14110 Condé-sur-Noireau
N° d'Imprimeur : 118976 - Dépôt légal : mai 2015 - *Imprimé en France*

www.ingramcontent.com/pod-product-compliance
Lightning Source LLC
LaVergne TN
LVHW010934061026
849535LV00007B/2386